THE EIGHT STEP HEALING PLAN

MICHAELA ROSE
NATURAL HEALTH CONSULTANT, D.N. MED

CONTENTS

INTRODUCTION

This is the story of my recovery, and hopefully it will be yours as well.

I'm a natural health consultant and health writer based in the UK. I have seen thousands of patients, over two decades involved in natural medicine, and now spend most of my time helping people to investigate unresolving illness and find ways to recover. My natural health career evolved because I suffered from a chronic illness myself and I couldn't get well. My usual techniques simply weren't working — at one point, I couldn't even tolerate medication and could only eat a few foods — so I had to try something drastic; I re-evaluated everything I knew and opened my mind to new ideas. And, eventually, I started recovering.

This book is the result of all that learning and experience and will take you through the journey I took to get well, in the hope that it might spark some new ways forward for you. I've collected the recurring concepts and treatment approaches that seem to work for most chronic illnesses — techniques that have helped me and my patients — and I'll show you how I used them, why and when. So, if you have a hypersensitivity illness, including chronic fatigue, fibromyalgia, multiple sensitivity, anxiety disorders, trauma-triggered illness, chronic pain —

especially headaches and muscular pain — and pre-menstrual syndrome (PMS), or you're just not getting better from something and want to give yourself the best shot at doing so, I hope that this book will help you.

Chronic illness takes many different forms, and this healing plan is designed to help no matter what your triggers are. Mine were mainly food-related. Perhaps yours are reactions to chemicals, electromagnetism, stress, even all of the above or something totally different. Whatever your symptoms, the steps in this book will help you.

You've probably spent a lot of time and energy worrying about your illness; it's now time to focus that energy instead on following this eight-step healing plan. But be warned, it will take time (a year or more), dedication and an open mind. Let's start with some context:

What happened to me?

I had a difficult start in life, with an alcoholic Mum resulting in me being in and out of care through early childhood. Mum committed suicide when I was 10 and I was taken into permanent care. The worst thing about it was that I was removed from any sense of familiarity, ripped from my known environment and my siblings; we were separated and kept apart and, to this day, I really don't know why! Suffice to say, it was tough, and I had to grow up very fast.

Despite all that — thanks in large part to the stable care of my foster home — I did really well at school, got a good degree in African, American and English Literature and developed a very successful career in natural medicine.

Health-wise, life has always been difficult, starting with bone, stomach and head pains as a child and polycystic ovary syndrome (PCOS) as a teenager. From my early twenties onwards, I have suffered food intolerance moving on to the ubiquitous irritable bowel syndrome (IBS), severe mouth/gum/jawbone pain, migraine, crushing chronic fatigue, restless legs, adrenal and hormonal dysfunction and chronic muscle pain

— to name only the main symptoms. I was finally left with around 20 foods I could eat and a sensitivity to the world in general.

My approach to getting well had to change drastically when I realised I couldn't follow any of my own patient protocols. I simply couldn't tolerate any supplements, meds, stuff on my skin, herbals, homeopathy or the foods I would normally suggest. I was suffering terrible mouth and migraine pain at the time and couldn't even tolerate painkillers. It was a nightmare.

I had done all the usual elimination diets, tried to lower toxicity, remove allergens, reduce inflammation, correct the gut, but nothing worked for long, if at all. I'd even invented the (Truly Gluten Free) (TGF) approach of dairy and grain free, gone autoimmune protocol (AIP) and eliminated every food — bar a few — and then couldn't get them back into my diet! I had to come up with a different strategy.

Turning my health around

The one good thing that came out of this very scary time was that it started me thinking about non-ingestive healing methods. I had to figure out what I could do to get myself well that didn't involve ingesting foods, meds or supplements. And I'd had enough of the 'cut it out' approach. I had very little left to cut out anyway. Even on fewer than 20 foods, my fatigue, mouth pain and migraine hadn't gone. I was leading a very depressing life and was terrified of losing more of my future. It needed to stop — but then, so did my symptoms. I needed a more positive approach.

So, I started writing down everything I found useful about non-ingestive healing methods and started blogging about Mind–Body medicine on my blog.

Since then, I have been researching and trialling various healing methods. This has been a huge learning curve and I'm excited to be able to share my discoveries with you.

My approach to chronic illness

I now specialise in trauma-triggered illness, central sensitivity syndrome and hypersensitivity disorders as well as gluten-related disorders—coeliac and non-coeliac gluten-sensitivity (NCGS)—using all the knowledge I've gained personally and with patients.

To get truly well from a persistent, unresolving chronic illness, of whatever type, we need to work on the brain and subconscious as well as — and sometimes before — we chase down the biochemistry with tests, meds and supplements. In fact, I tend nowadays to ask people to do the healing work first and then see what they are left with that needs fixing biochemically.

You can certainly shore up the body and improve symptoms with physical/biochemical treatments, but long term you are not achieving healing.

If you put your body into the healing state it needs, change the way the brain is thinking about illness and remove the subconscious triggers, it has the power to turn itself around without so much biochemical work. This is tough for a biochemist-trained medical nutritionist to admit, but I like to say I used my head to get well, which is pretty much true, because I had nothing else left to use!

My clinical approach nowadays is to combine functional nutritional medicine with cognitive and brain retraining (neuroplasticity techniques) and subconscious work. This gets to the root cause of illnesses that aren't responding to normal treatment and changes it.

The Healing Plan

People ask what I did to get well, and this healing plan is essentially my response. I have analysed — from the 47 different approaches I tried over a three-year period — what worked and what didn't, and prepared a step-by-step guide for you to follow.

During this process, we'll start by calming your hypersensitive amygdala — your stress response — so that you can start healing. We'll examine the emotional triggers, neural pathways and unhelpful beliefs that are contributing to your chronic illness. Following these eight steps to healing will also change your subconscious and conscious mind simultaneously. We'll explore techniques that will enable you to release and process buried emotions and trauma, and then rewire your brain with new, healthier patterns.

Finally, we find a new identity and re-enter the world as a well person. Through all that, we support ourselves nutritionally and, at the end, deal with any physical symptoms that are left.

Although I've explained these steps separately, you'll probably do several of them concurrently and they'll build as you go along until suddenly — almost without you really noticing — you find yourself much better.

Of course, no two individuals are the same, so this book can only ever show you how I did it. I'll recommend some things for you to try, explain why they might be the right approach for you and what order it might be best to work through them in.

Good luck following your healing path, I'm rooting for you!

Micki Rose

1

Before You Start Following This Plan

Disclaimer

This book is based on my opinion as a natural health consultant only. The information contained in this book is not a substitute for a consultation with your own doctor. It should not take the place of medical professional advice in any way and should not be relied upon as such. It is designed to give you a base understanding of a health issue and pointers to help you forward toward a resolution.

Always check with your doctor or nutritionist before making any changes to your diet, medicines or supplements. Always exercise common sense. I accept no responsibility whatsoever for illness arising out of failure to seek medical advice from a doctor.

Important

Remember: always check with your health practitioner or GP before starting anything new; also continue to work with your chosen support team during treatment. Be careful with new supplements, especially if you are taking any medicines, are pregnant, or trying to conceive, or have high blood pressure.

2

How to Use This Book

THIS IS A SELF-HELP PROGRAMME, and you should follow it under the care of your chosen health professionals.

This book outlines the eight key steps I took to turn my health around. It was a massive learning curve — and one where I had to suspend disbelief quite a lot — but it worked. My genuine hope is that it will help you too. I will explain what I did to recover and suggest resources for you to follow. Work with what you learn, and with your health professionals, to achieve your aims.

Read it through first, and then take it one step at a time.

I know you are desperate to skip through and get going, but trust me, it will save you loads of confusion if you start at the beginning and read this plan through completely. Reading it a couple of times is part of your treatment; all will be revealed!

So, read the steps all the way through. Don't start working through the steps or following advice; just read. Scoff, pooh-pooh, faint and whoop as you like. Some of the steps I suggest may seem fantastical, but they have worked, so do keep an open mind. Then, get a pad and pen, read it through again and this time, take notes. You'll then be ready to start working through Step One.

It's easy to get overwhelmed so take it at your own pace and go as slowly as you need to. You don't have to do everything, just do what you can. A lot of this is instinctive so, if you feel like doing something — or not doing it — trust your instinct as it usually knows more than you do. I've offered up several choices of techniques in the steps but don't feel that you have to use all of them. I like to chop and change techniques, however, you may prefer to simply stick with one. Again, go with whatever feels right to you.

Remember, in natural medicine, there is a general rule that you will need one month's treatment for every year you have been ill. Each person is different and there are no guarantees, of course. But, if you think that most chronic illnesses take many years to develop it is very likely going to take a good while to get yourself well — and that's fine. You'll see that one of our first steps is to stop pushing it. (Hard, I know. Been there!)

So, starting now, think ahead and imagine how you want to be health-wise in a few months or a year. Get a really detailed picture, using all your senses, in your mind. That's what you're aiming for. Keep it in your mind as you go along.

Now, it's time to learn more about the rollercoaster ride of chronic disease.

I know that this section is quite long but please do read it through carefully. It is really important that you understand what is going on before you start work.

I will then take you through an overview of the eight steps to healing.

Please also read these carefully. It is important and helpful to have some idea of what you are going to do before you start to do it.

3

The Chronic Disease Recovery Rollercoaster

Healing is certainly not linear or straightforward; I felt like I was jumping around all over the place during my own journey. But, with the benefit of hindsight, I actually realised I had followed a known pathway to recovery. I wish I'd known what to expect and what was going on when my own healing journey started; at least I can share what I now know with you!

There are several fundamental principles involved in recovering from a chronic illness, so let's look at those:

1) Conditions are multi-factorial and you need a multi-factorial approach to get better.

There's usually a lot going on — affecting multiple body systems and organs — by the time someone becomes chronically ill. The focus of treatment is usually the physical body, chasing down individual conditions and alleviating symptoms. That usually helps — to a point —

but it doesn't undo the chronic condition; people might get better to a degree, or they might relapse entirely.

This is probably because no-one has addressed the other levels of the illness. What's going on in the subconscious, the energetic system, the brain and cognition? What's the social context, such as family and work? How strong is that person spiritually, how connected are they, how well supported are they? We pay lip-service to all that, but I learned that in unresolving cases there needs to be much, much more emphasis put on these elements of the illness.

I spent years focusing only on the physical, biochemical aspects of the body. Only latterly did I realise the importance of beliefs, brain neuroplasticity and cognitive Pavlovian habits. However, it was only when I also focused on my spiritual strength, emotional resilience and understanding, as well as the underlying trauma, the environment around me, and the people I was with, and dovetailed all that with the physical and subconscious work, that healing actually took place.

So, a multi-factorial illness usually has causes and exacerbators on several levels — it is rarely only physical. And, to get well, you have to work on all of those levels (either simultaneously or in the right order for you). Which brings me on to:

2) Recovery or healing is not linear, you go back and forth, up and down, stalling and motoring all the time.

Just knowing that and accepting it takes a huge weight off you during the recovery process, trust me! If you're expecting that it won't be a straightforward A to B process, and that there will be ups and downs, you'll be much more prepared. I wasn't, so I kept re-traumatising myself all the time, thinking: "Here we go again, I'm never going to get well, it doesn't matter what I do."

It can be really useful to work out where you are on your recovery path using some classic healing models. Understanding if you're still in crisis mode, or if you're stabilised, or if you're in one of the other stages, will help you choose the approach and treatment options that are most likely to help you at that particular point.

For example, it's no good trying to do a biochemical detox, gut protocol or even a brain-retraining programme if you are in crisis; it'll just make you worse (I know from personal experience!) Equally, physical therapy is not what you need if you're going through the realisation stage; when you suddenly understand that there is no going back fully to the old you or old life. (Don't worry, I'll talk you through exactly what you need and when, later in this programme.)

Fundamentally, your body can only work with the energy and resources it has at each point. It's no good forcing it because ultimately it will go at its own pace no matter what you do! The trick is to relax, listen very carefully and let it take over. Which brings me on to the next fundamental principle:

3) Your body knows how to heal; all you need to do is give it the chance.

One of the things that got me through the worst times was remembering my naturopathic training and that the body has more power, knowledge and healing ability than we can ever hope to understand.

Our job is quite simple: we need to put our body and mind into a healing state rather than a disease state and then let it get on with showing us what to do next. Let it heal. It knows far more than you do, and certainly more than any practitioner come to that.

Of course, everyone's needs are different and that's why it's important to bear all three principles in mind during your recovery. You'll learn to listen to the stage you are at and do what the body needs next. Don't force it!

Now we've covered the principles, it's time to look at two excellent models that explain the recovery journey.

Patricia Fennell's Four Phase Model

This model — described in detail in Fennell's book, 'Managing Chronic Illness' — is fabulous. Fennell specialises in chronic disease, and she developed her model to try and make sense of what her patients were going through. The full model is complex, so I've created this simple overview to map out the journey to recovery. Reading the phases will assist you in working out where you are in your illness and recovery — which is helpful for understanding what levels of intervention from Klinghardt et al (see further in this chapter) might be right for you at any given moment.

I've interpreted Fennell's four phases in the context of the illnesses that I've seen and experienced; it may not be how she originally saw it, so I hope she'll forgive me for that!

Phase One: Crisis

This first phase is about realising that although you may look fine, you are actually quite seriously or debilitatingly ill. The chances are that you will have seen many healthcare professionals trying to get a diagnosis, but you have been ignored, disbelieved (even by people close to you) or misdiagnosed. Perhaps nothing shows up on tests. You might get a few answers and start working on those, but you realise this isn't going away anytime soon. Suddenly, you see yourself as an 'ill person', which is traumatising in itself.

You're probably spending lots of time desperately googling your symptoms, looking for relief. Some may look for spiritual relief, others may turn to deadening tactics like drinking, drugs, and the one I chose — ignoring it!

The main task of this phase for you (and your doctors, caregivers, family and friends) is to lower the immediate pain and trauma. Sadly, what happens is people get traumatised, don't get the answers or support they really need and the person continues in crisis for far too long.

Phase Two: Stabilisation

After some time, you move into this phase, experiencing what have now become familiar symptoms and feeling a bit better; or at least, managing better. You are probably trying different interventions — usually one or two at a time — and making some progress but relapsing a lot and wondering if you are ever going to get better. This becomes depressing, obviously.

You are hankering after your old life when you were well. You keep trying to do things you did before the illness and realising that you can't. That, again, is traumatising and frustrating. You still feel in crisis a lot, but some days you are hopeful. You may get very excited about a treatment then, when it doesn't work as you hoped, get low and feel a failure. It becomes difficult to see any success and you start to spiral into despair, becoming more and more depressed by the rollercoaster ride.

Cognitively, your brain is becoming set in failure grooves. Mentally, you're trying your hardest not to act or look ill all the time, trying to not be a burden to your family. Meanwhile, you're constantly researching, thinking and acting on your illness and interventions.

Physically, you will be shattered by it all. While you might manage to juggle life, family, commitments and work, it's certainly taking a toll on you. You start to feel really depressed, fearful of the illness, the symptoms, of the future and wonder how you're going to cope.

The main task here is to stop trying to get back to your old life, to accept that you have an illness for whatever reason and to stop fighting; to stabilise your mental state. You need to let go of the fight and put your body into a healing state rather than one at war with itself.

Phase Three: Resolution

Phase three may bring a plateau of symptoms, or perhaps you may be better but have relapses. At this point, you've learned how your illness behaves and how the world responds to it. You've also finally learned that you can't fully be the person that you used to be before you got ill. This can be a devastating perception; one that can make you experience a dark night of the soul.

However, I see it as a grieving process followed by a rising of the phoenix; you have to hit rock bottom before you can come back up as someone stronger. It is an emotionally tough stage — during it you may feel out of control and lost — but, eventually, the lights flicker on again and you begin to think: "If I can't be the old me, who will I be then?"

That's quite exciting. You might not be able to do all the stuff you used to do, but you can certainly do some of it, plus some different stuff. Acceptance is the key here. When you have accepted a situation and stopped fighting it, you can move forwards; whilst you're still fighting, you can't.

Your task during this phase is to develop a new sense of self that fits with you, at this point, and brings together all that you have learned so far.

Phase Four: Integration

In phase four, you may experience a plateau of symptoms or periodic relapses, but you're now able to integrate parts of your old self (from before the illness) with the person you are now. Your task in this phase is to keep finding ways to express the new you and start to live life again. It's a life where illness may well play a part — even a big part — but it is not the be-all and end-all. You have other stuff in your life to focus on and be part of, and you enjoy life again.

The ultimate aim is to position your illness within a larger life framework; to have a whole, complete, new type of life, of which illness is only one part. I know if you are reading this in phase one, you're probably thinking that will never be the case for you. But, it will be. You can and will get there, trust me!

Summary

Fennell's model is brilliant for giving you an overview of the stages of illness. Even if you don't get any of it yet — nor accept it because you're still in the crisis phase and can't see out of it — you will start to see yourself move back and forth through these stages and that, ultimately, makes you feel a little bit more in control.

As well as 'Managing Chronic Illness', you can also read more on Fennell's Four Phase Model in her book, 'The Chronic Illness Workbook' — it's rather technical in places, but I enjoyed it.

Dr Dietrich Klinghardt's Five Levels of Healing

This second model shows how disease — and therefore healing — happens on several levels. It reflects the multi-factorial nature of chronic disease and the work you need to do on several areas, often simultaneously, to achieve real, lasting recovery.

As before, I have paraphrased the levels to show you how it works for the type of cases I see.

Level One: The Physical Body

This is our foundation: the cells, organs, structures; the biochemics of the physical body. When you're carrying out activities like testing nutrient issues or adrenal fatigue, having massage or taking medication, you are working on this level. We tend to focus on the physical body because it's the most obvious *us*.

Level Two: The Energy Body

We are electrical beings; magnetised, energetic and totally in touch with all the other energies around us, even if we can't feel them. Think of our nervous system, meridians, auras and circadian rhythms. I also think of this level as the Emotional Body, the *us* that feels things like anger, or fear, and is affected by trauma.

At this level, you might be bringing emotions to the surface and acknowledging them, rather than suppressing them, and working to achieve more of a balance. Tools that you might use at this stage include acupuncture, yoga, Bowen therapy or QI Gong. (See glossary for detail.)

Level Three: The Mental Body

This comprises our thoughts, beliefs, perceptions, learned behaviours, conditioned responses, memories, associations on both the conscious and subconscious levels. Here, you're working very much on the subconscious with approaches like hypnotherapy, cognitive behavioural therapy (CBT) or psychotherapy.

Level Four: The Intuitive Body

On this level, we start opening up to our intuition; we note our dreams, visions, thoughts that arise in meditation, and use it all to find the next steps to healing. It took me a long time to accept the concept of this dream body but, in the end, this is the level that made the most difference for me in practical, getting-better terms. I nearly choked when

I first saw this body explained — I had thought it was just me using my dreams and intuition to tell me how to get well.

Level Five: The Spiritual Body

This is the highest level for a reason; it refers to bliss, a sense of knowingness, an awareness of how you fit into the rest of the universe. I experienced it quite early on during deep meditation and, quite frankly, the power of it scared me. I suddenly knew I had this massive power within me; I didn't know what it was, but it gradually grew from that first day. From being initially scared of it, now I am more scared I will lose it! Working on this level comes through prayer, deep meditation, quiet contemplation and being in nature.

Summary

These five levels encompass our entire bodies; you don't have to move through them in any order and may actually go in and out of them several times during your path to recovery. It doesn't really matter where you start but, both for me and from what I have read, upset and dysfunction in the higher levels only show themselves as physical symptoms in level one after quite a while.

That does indicate that the best place to start is not the physical body (level one), but somewhere higher up. When I realised I was ill, I started looking at level two (of course, I didn't know it was level two then!), wondering if my physical illness was actually an emotional one? I unearthed a lot of hurt and began to meditate as a way of calming myself down.

The soul meditation was so helpful that I tipped into level five within just a few weeks and got my bliss moment. From then on, I worked on all the lower levels using hypnotherapy, brain retraining, emotional freedom techniques (EFT), eye movement desensitisation and retraining (EMDR),

Qi Gong and lots more besides, but I always felt the strength of the level five stuff there with me.

I have seen people go up, down and all over through this model. You don't need to plan anything but just being aware of what levels there are, and what you do to help yourself in them, can be immensely helpful. And, if you trust your body, it will lead you through your own recovery path anyway.

Finally, clearing stuff on higher levels can effectively augment, spark or negate the need for healing on lower levels. For example, if you work on level three and change a neural pathway with brain retraining, you can change the fear (level two) of a symptom and then the symptom itself goes or changes on level one. Working on levels three and four, with my dreams and hypnotherapy imagining the rebuilding of damaged pathways and synapses in my brain, sparked an actual physical detox, evidenced by very yellow bowel movements and a disappearance of my level one migraine.

You can find out more about Klinghardt's work at: http://klinghardtinstitute.com/ and his website also hosts two great summary tables of Dr Klinghardt's Five Levels of Healing — here and here — that clearly show you the model.

4

What's Causing Our Chronic Illness?

Being chronically ill is in itself exhausting, stressful and frustrating. So, understanding why we might be ill in the first place can be really empowering; once we know what might be contributing to our illness, we can see a path towards addressing it. Many of us with unrelenting chronic illnesses share several underlying traits and we'll look at each one in detail in this section:

- A brain that's over-sensitive to what it wrongly interprets as danger
- A brain that amplifies pain
- Negative thought patterns and beliefs that subconsciously reinforce the unhelpful grooves in your brain
- Problems with the gut, and other barriers

The majority of those factors reference the brain, which some people find surprising and upsetting because they think the inference is that their pain isn't real. That's not the case. Of course, your pain is real — I've experienced it myself, so I do understand — however, your brain may be contributing to your illness and symptoms far more than you realise.

The Overly-Sensitive Brain

We'll start by looking at the oldest part of our brains to understand its role in our health.

The Amygdala and the 'Stuck On-Switch'

The amygdala is the so-called lizard brain, and it's a tiny, almond-shaped part of the brain with a very important task. It controls how we react to our environment — our fight-or-flight response. But, unfortunately, it's not very bright! This reaction was vital when we needed to be constantly alert for sabre-toothed tigers and other threats in the Neolithic world. It's no doubt what kept us alive, but, it's not so useful when it starts perceiving danger in harmless things, for example: food, noise or going out.

The Thalamus-Amygdala Stress Response

The thalamus is like a switchboard in the brain. It takes information from all our senses (except for the sense of smell, which bypasses it) and sends it to the appropriate part of the brain for processing, while firing up the amygdala to do a risk assessment of the situation. The amygdala is constantly learning from your experiences, so that it can protect you. Unfortunately, that means that if you have a reaction to something — no matter how innocuous the trigger is — it will recognise that food, substance, person or even situation as a danger. Then, every time you encounter it, your amygdala reacts even more strongly and quickly to protect you. This stress response releases a cascade of body chemicals—including adrenaline and cortisol — which leads to other reactions, like increased blood pressure, racing heart, flushing and shaking.

Of course, this response is subconscious, but, if it happens too often eventually our stress response switch gets stuck in the on position and we become hypersensitive. The constant stimuli — seeing/tasting/thinking about your thing — triggers your thalamus, which gives the amygdala an even stronger signal, and you get a larger stress response. This leads you to think about the problem more, and the reactions become ever greater and more frequent. So, an everyday occurrence — perhaps a row with your partner, a barking dog, a noisy neighbour — can escalate into something that makes you feel stressed or inappropriately angry. We feel overwhelmed, which just feeds more into the amygdala sensitisation and it becomes a vicious circle.

When the body is in a state of hypervigilance, and the stress response is constantly triggered, it's harmful to our health. The floods of hormones, cytokines and body complexes can lead to chronic illness, high inflammation, poor immunity, adrenal fatigue and much more. The muscles tense, digestion slows down considerably, the adrenaline heightens the sensitivity of the brain and makes things worse, plus you release sugar into the bloodstream in case you need more fuel. I'm certain that this constant firing is a key reason why most food or chemical-sensitives are so adrenally fatigued; they just can't keep up with demand. It's no wonder that eventually leads to illness.

Genetic and Methylation Problems

Some people have a genetically-programmed issue with the amygdala that can make them highly sensitive. Single nucleotide polymorphisms (SNiPs) are the most common type of genetic variation between people, and there are two key ones that you can look for:

The Sensitivity Gene: 5HTTLPR. This one seems to be mostly related to serotonin processing so resilience may be lower generally in people with this SNiP, and they simply don't cope as well with stress.

The Stress Vulnerability Gene: NR3C1. Cortisol is our flight or fight hormone and is raised during acute stress. If you have the stress vulnerability gene, then cortisol stays in your system for longer; this means that you effectively react to stress more than normal people.

Just because you have these genes, you're not guaranteed to have these problems; the genes first have to be triggered or switched on by a process called methylation. The amygdala releases a specific protein, which triggers a cascade, which turns on the genes that control the stress response at cellular levels. Many people have methylation defects, this eventually leads to increased inflammation and cellular ageing.

It seems that when the brain is developing in childhood, it is particularly vulnerable to this process. If a child suffers trauma — such as a major (to them) stress, or an extreme reaction — then this process of methylation can go awry. That could include the disabling of the genes that control the stress response appropriately, or the sensitivity genes getting triggered; the end result is that our stress-response switch gets stuck on.

This stopped me in my tracks, as I didn't exactly have a great childhood. Could there be a link there to my hypersensitivity?

Adverse Childhood Events and Memories (ACE)

I started researching how Adverse Childhood Events (ACE) affect our future physiology. The more ACEs a person suffers, the more likely they are to have future illness. We'll calculate your ACE score later on your journey, and look at their impact on your health, as it will be key to your healing. And if you're thinking: "Ah, but I never suffered any trauma" — bear with me. Everyone says that!

The original research on ACEs found surprising and significant links between major childhood trauma and later adult chronic illness: obesity, lung disease, stroke and heart disease. It's a huge, evolving area of medicine, covering numerous types of trauma, and has been linked heavily to conditions including autoimmune disease, depression, anxiety, suicide tendency, fibromyalgia, chronic fatigue and hypersensitivity disorders.

The statistics are staggering: people with two or more ACEs have a 70% higher risk of developing a TH1 dominant immune disease (for example: Coeliac disease, Type 1 Diabetes, Crohn's, Hashimoto's, psoriasis, multiple sclerosis) than someone with none. Similarly, there is an 80% higher risk of getting a TH2 dominant immune disease (for example: allergies, asthma, colitis, inflammatory bowel disease, eczema and lupus).

Perhaps you don't think you suffered any trauma as a child? Many people assume that trauma only refers to things like violence, physical and sexual abuse. However, the definition is wider than that, and also refers to emotional or physical neglect, being put down, feeling alone, bullied, fearful or unsafe. And it doesn't just refer to childhood trauma either — because adult or so-called later-life trauma can have exactly the same effect — it's just that if a child suffers trauma of some kind as their brain is developing (before they're ten years old), it is much more likely to cause a hyperactive amygdala: the stuck on-switch.

Most people have had some trauma, of course, and that's normal; it helps us build resilience to life. The issue comes when a person is habitually and often subtly (or not so subtly) traumatised that starts to cause actual brain, hormone and genetic changes. Indeed, I discovered my own chronic illness — including migraine, chronic fatigue, chronic body-wide sensitivity — was mostly caused by childhood trauma.

At first, I had no idea that my childhood experiences were behind my illness; I was in my forties when I became chronically ill. But the ACEs are buried until we are ready to deal with them. Even if we don't recognise them, or think about them consciously anymore, they're still there dripping like a leaky tap and leading to later illness. Apparently, this is most likely to trigger by your thirties onwards, and the most common illnesses include IBS (my first illness) and migraine (my most recent illness).

I felt a bit shell-shocked by this. Could my hypersensitivity really go back to my traumatic childhood? I'd always assumed that food was the problem, but perhaps it was nothing to do with it. Had I just focused, subconsciously, on food as the source of my problems, maybe even because I was a nutritionist and talked about it all day, every day? As a trained nutritionist, I found it hard to accept. But, I'd promised to keep an open mind to whatever the universe revealed to me; even so it still took three diagnoses of post-traumatic stress disorder (PTSD) and ACE illness — and almost three years — to believe that my illness wasn't just physical.

The Memory

Another part of our old brain is the hippocampus, which controls memory and how you deal with emotion. Scientists have found that ACEs and the stress response triggers a hormone that affects the hippocampus, which then under-develops. The results of that can include poor memory and trouble dealing with emotions: either being hyper-emotional or cold in some way. I am certainly the former; I can cry at anything and I feel things — especially other people's pain — far too sensitively.

More than that, I was told once by a neurologist that I had a dissociative memory condition, meaning my brain had shut off memories that were too painful to bear. I couldn't recall anything from childhood bar a few memories; it has improved over time but not by much. Apparently — especially in adolescence — the brain can block the amygdala and hippocampus, or certainly dampen their responses, as a kind of coping mechanism. You feel less, and you recall less. Neuroscientists now believe that this is a special form of neuroplasticity where we change our brains. That knowledge gave me hope, as plasticity works both ways, and I realised that I could undo it.

Of course, ACEs don't explain every case — but for the last year or so, I've been asking my patients and followers if they had any major stress or trauma in childhood. The numbers are huge, and I'm now much more surprised when someone says no than when they say yes. Certainly, these illnesses aren't all in the mind, but the mental component of them mustn't be underestimated.

Central Sensitivity Syndrome (CSS) or Sustained Sympathetic Upregulation (SSU)

Next, let's consider a sensitivity syndrome which may be playing a key part in our chronic illness by causing our switch to stay on. Central Sensitivity Syndrome (CSS) — is talked about a lot in the fibromyalgia world and its sufferers have higher than normal sensitivity settings. Much of the research, and the way it is talked about, is to do with pain, however you can swap the word pain for 'food', 'light', 'person' or whatever your personal trigger is. I've heard CSS described, rather brilliantly, as a disease of over-sensitivity to threats; it's our stuck-on switch yet again seeing danger in innocuous things.

CSS is controlled by a brain-amplified activity, not by inflammation or immune activity in the local area. This is important, we used to think that all pain came from damage or inflammation in local tissues, but that's now disproven in many cases. So, the pain is still local in examples like sciatica (nerve compression) and wounds, however there are now known to be centralised pain conditions — like fibromyalgia (FM), IBS, headaches, even interstitial cystitis and vulvodynia — where the pain is a brain-amplification problem and not local inflammation.

There's another, very similar, condition that doesn't focus on pain quite so much: Sustained Sympathetic Upregulation (SSU). It's described as a condition of neurological hypervigilance that causes chronic reactivity and discomfort, and it covers any cause or condition where the brain seems to amplify pain. However, I'll use CSS to refer to both conditions; just be mindful that we're not only talking about pain.

The key message here is that we can work on the leaky gut, inflammation and immune reactions all we want, but, certainly in some people, it is actually this hypervigilance we should be working on. Of course, physiological things may be happening as well, but if they're not responding to the normal treatment protocols, we need to look here instead.

These are some of the main conditions associated with CSS:

- Fibromyalgia syndrome (FM)
- Chronic Fatigue Syndrome (CFS)
- Multiple Chemical Sensitivity (MCS)
- Irritable Bowel Syndrome (IBS)
- Migraine
- Frequent Tension-Type Headaches (TTH)
- Premenstrual Syndrome (PMS)
- Food Hypersensitivity
- Stimuli Hypersensitivity
- Interstitial Cystitis
- Vulvodynia
- Temporomandibular Joint Pain (TMJ)
- Dental pain
- Visceral pain (thoracic, abdominal or pelvic pain)
- Some other psychiatric disorders can occur with CSS too, including depression, Obsessive Compulsive Disorder (OCD), bipolar disorder, Post-Traumatic Stress Disorder (PTSD), General Anxiety Disorder (GAD) and panic attacks.

How many illnesses have you had on that list? I've had nine of them at various stages of my life.

How do you know if you have CSS?

If you've had the following, then you're likely to be classified as a CSS sufferer:

- Pain, or symptoms in several different areas of the body, or pain that moves about from day to day. You may also have had several different types of pain throughout life, often starting in childhood or teens.
- I'd actually never really thought of my problem as pain, until I did this exercise. I had bone pain, headaches and stomach ache in childhood, then severe PMS. In my twenties, I had PMS, IBS, neck and back pain, then in my thirties: IBS, restless legs, headaches, ear pain, neck and back pain. My forties saw migraine, throat closure, mouth and jaw pain.
- Your condition vacillates a lot, and is unpredictable, so you never know when a flare-up is going to happen.
- Abnormal pain — pain that's somehow heightened or always present in some way.
- For me, it hurt to wear a bra, points on my head always hurt when pressed, bed sheets and clothes can hurt, sometimes even hugs hurt!
- Pain is often nerve-type — that is, gnawing, burning, stabbing or deep — rather than sharp.
- Other symptoms could include fatigue, sleep issues and memory difficulties. You may have already noticed that this sounds like fibromyalgia but do understand that FM is part of the CSS spectrum; many hypersensitivity conditions will also have these other symptoms.
- Often sensitive to other elements like light, temperature, noise and smells.
- Tend to suffer from depression, distress, anxiety: not least because of the pain, but also because the same neurotransmitters involved in the amplification process affect mood.

If you suspect that you have CSS and would like to know more about it, then do read the article on my website – https://purehealthclinic.co.uk.

So, why does the brain amplify pain?

There are two main pathways to pain in the brain and central nervous system; these either increase pain signalling or decrease it, and both are controlled by specific neurotransmitters (NTs). Someone may have too much glutamate and Substance P — which are excitatory NTs — and not enough of the inhibitory neurotransmitters like serotonin, dopamine or noradrenaline/norepinephrine. Whenever I test someone's neurotransmitters, if I see high glutamate then I look even harder for clues to a CSS illness.

These neurotransmitters are also involved in various mood disorders; this means many CSS sufferers are also going to suffer with, or have their sensitivity heightened by, conditions like chronic anxiety, depression, trauma. Again, I see this in my own life; I believe my early life trauma caused PTSD, which turned my amplifier up and lead to me being over-sensitive to normal stimuli.

If you'd like to know more about CSS, there's an excellent video by the expert Dr Daniel Clauw, and here are some further facts to consider:

- Women, especially of menstruating age, are one-and-a-half to two times more likely to have CSS. Pain is worse just before menstruation.
- Genetics are involved (there is a small list of the genes involved in the Clauw video if you want to check for SNiPs).
- CSS is thought to be triggered, or exacerbated, by:
- Stress
- Emotional: for example, fear, anger, anxiety
- Psychological: for example, bereavement, divorce, financial crisis
- Physical: for example, infection or inflammation

- Injury, especially if the pain from it continues for more than three months (for example, whiplash).
- As we've already seen, ACEs (and other adverse events in the past) can be a huge contributory factor.

Over time, the consequences of chronic pain and sensitivity make things worse and we go into a spiral. We become more and more distressed by what's happening to us, we isolate ourselves more and we don't sleep well. Often, we get stuck in behavioural ruts that aggravate the problem, like doing too much on good days and overwhelming ourselves. I'll explain what you can do, if you think you have CSS, later in this section. For now, let's look at other factors that might be contributing to our chronic illness.

Brain Neuroplasticity

Neuroplasticity refers to the brain's amazing ability to adapt and change. When we repeat the same subconscious thought patterns, beliefs and associations, it creates deep neural pathways (also called grooves) in our brains; these get deeper every time we think the same things. Our thoughts literally change our brains. Neuroscientists believe that if the thoughts are negative then those unhelpful thoughts become self-fulfilling; we become more and more fearful of our triggers and react more strongly to them. Happily, we can use neuroplasticity to our advantage, using positive thoughts to create better grooves, and we'll explore this later.

Ill Health and the Gut

A decline in health usually starts in the digestive system. Stress lowers our ability to digest, eventually meaning that we can't absorb nutrients properly, and the poor nutrient levels cause every system and organ of the body to under-function. Bacterial and other infections like Helicobacter pylori (H. pylori) that can cause peptic ulcers, candida and other parasites have more of a chance to take hold as there's invariably not enough stomach acid to kill them; your enzyme production drops, you don't digest food effectively any more, and that leftover food encourages further bacterial growth. Your microbiome in the gut changes, leading to your whole body to change at a very basic level; your ability to control inflammation, cellular change and repair mechanisms is affected.

Eventually, you start getting symptoms in those various under-nourished and inflamed organs and cells. You start to worry about how you are feeling, and to dread what will happen next, and that stress takes us into the feedback loop of the thalamus and amygdala. Worry causes more worry.

A Link with The Barriers?

If we accept that our basic problem is a malfunctioning protective mechanism (our stress response), then could that translate to other, more tangible, protective mechanisms in the body? Specifically, the barriers: the blood-brain barrier, the lung barrier, the gut barrier and the skin. There's a protein that's released by the amygdala when stimulated, and high levels of it are found in the skin of people with conditions like psoriasis and eczema.

We all know skin conditions are affected by stress, don't we? Well, why would other inner skin like the gut, lungs, and brain-barriers be any different just because you can't see them? I theorise, of course, but what if the on-switch causing hypervigilance is actually translating into barriers that have become hypervigilant (and likely inflamed) too?

5

What Can We Do About Our Chronic Illness?

As we've just seen, there may be various factors contributing to your chronic illness. This plan will explain what you can do to address them, so we'll look at tackling the original triggers — like ACEs, stress and reactions — to turn your stuck-on switch, off, as well as undoing the learned behaviours, beliefs and conditioned responses that your subconscious brain is clinging on to.

Calming it down

When your amygdala is stuck-on (misinterpreting every signal as a threat), and your brain is amplifying the pain, your immediate therapy should be about soothing yourself. When your brain thinks you're safe, your pain levels reduce. We're going to work to calm the amygdala; if we think of it as a small child, we can help it grow up in a different way.

Mirror Neurons

This is a theory — albeit controversial — that seeing and hearing others do something helps you build your own similar neural pathways in the brain. Of course, it's much more complex than that and, if you're interested in learning more, there's an excellent article about it in the Journal of Natural Science, Biology and Medicine. I found reading people's recovery stories — whether in books, or on internet groups and forums — extremely helpful and inspiring and this will form part of your therapy too.

Changing the brain: Neuroplasticity

Up until relatively recently, brain scientists felt we had a static brain and genetic make-up that we couldn't change.

Now, neuroscientists know that our brains are pretty fluid and can be changed quite significantly. We are not set in stone and we can indeed change the hand we have been dealt. It takes effort and time, but it can be done.

Neuroplasticity is one of the keys to your healing, and we'll explore it in much more depth later. For now, remember that if we think the same thoughts, have the same fears and do the same things over and over again, we build neuroplastic grooves that become deeper and stronger, and more and more automatic over time. However, we can use the same techniques to create new grooves and to make the old, unhelpful ones more shallow.

Not only can we change the brain grooves, we can change the gene methylation. If we accept that negative events, feelings and thoughts messed up the gene methylation in the first place, then it's not too far a stretch to accept that positive events, feelings, images and thoughts can do the opposite, is it?

If you remember, when our stress response (also known as the sympathetic response) triggers, it releases a whole load of hormones and internal chemicals that over time will cause some kind of chronic illness. However, if we trigger the parasympathetic (calming) response, the body releases a whole different set of complexes which are healing, protective and cellularly anti-ageing. So, we'll work later on finding parasympathetic-response triggers that work for us as individuals and start calming our systems down.

Revealing and dealing with buried trauma

We'll investigate any ACE disorders or traumas that are contributing to your illness. Revealing these emotions is intense work, and we'll cover how to support yourself during it, and how to process what comes up.

To summarise, we're going to learn to:

- Calm the amygdala and turn our switches off
- Trigger parasympathetic response, rather than stress response
- Encourage correct gene methylation
- Uncover and process any ACE disorders, memories, emotions or past events that are contributing to our condition
- Unpick any unhelpful beliefs or conditioned responses and, instead, use positive beliefs to create helpful, new neural pathways
- Encourage social, cultural and spiritual connection in support of getting well
- Build a new identity and image of ourselves and reintegrate so we can lead a good life despite of, whilst managing, or after our illness has gone

6

Overview of the Eight Steps

This healing plan splits broadly into two main types of step:

1. Calming the system down with parasympathetic techniques such as passive meditation, acceptance, heart meditation. This must be done first so that the system is ready for the next part:

2. Dynamic or active healing methods such as brain-retraining, neuroplasticity, visualisation and emotional healing.

I'll talk you through WHAT each of the steps are, and WHY they're so important, before I show you HOW to do them. That's because, if you're anything like me, you're desperate to get your life back on track. And my desperation meant that, at first, I often leapt ahead, missing out important things on the way.

I was too quick to jump into the healing work; doing it before my body was ready actually set back my recovery. However, once I calmed my system down, I was able to get on with the change work. So, your task now is to read and understand the steps ~~now~~ and I'll tell you exactly how to work them a little later!

Overview of Step One: Assess Your Immediate Nutritional and Medication Needs

You need to review which biochemical nutrition, herbs, homeopathy and meds to use at the very start of your healing journey, if you can tolerate them. This ensures that you've got a supportive protocol that keeps you nourished and will help you manage your symptoms. You'll review these needs again at the end of your journey. However, many people focus on their nutrition and medication without doing the healing work that is so central to this programme. Do not fixate on this step, to the exclusion of the others, otherwise the programme will not work properly for you.

When it's time to work this step, I'll talk you through examining your dietary and supplementary needs. The idea is that you remove any allergens and healing blockers from your diet while you are unwell, and then reintroduce these foods when you're better.

Most people with chronic illness, especially those with a gluten-related disorder or gut issue, will be malabsorbing and are usually on pretty restricted diets already. So, it's important to get the right supplements to help you maintain nutrient levels and reduce the risk of your restricted diet leading to other nutrient deficiency-related issues.

Also, anyone under chronic stress and especially anyone who is hypersensitive is running at top speed internally all the time. Can you imagine how much nutrient density your body needs just to keep up? Far more than normal, at a time when you can't get enough.

The right nutrition will help allay a lot of extra issues. The calming and healing work that we're going to do should ultimately lead to a lower need for so many nutrients and ensure better absorption.

Summary

You need to support yourself with nutrition and functional medicine at the start, throughout and at the end of your journey, but in quite different ways (and I'll explain them as we go). Proper nutrition helps lower your symptoms, which will help you to cope better. Nutrition and functional medicine supports your healing plan but is only part of the process; do not neglect the other steps!

Overview of Step Two: Accept and Forgive

Before you can move towards healing, you have to first accept there is a problem. Obviously, you already know there is a problem, because you are suffering, but it goes deeper than that. There is a difference between knowing something at an intellectual level, to accepting it at an emotional level.

I would constantly scan my body, always worrying and questioning myself: "Will I still be OK for that event this weekend?" "When will I feel better?" It was exhausting. I know a lot of people feel the same; constantly worrying, dealing with their fear, feeling they were fighting a battle.

I had spent years hoping and praying that one day this would all be over and that I would be better. When I suddenly realised that this was actually a real illness — and that there didn't seem to be anything I could do about it, no matter how hard I tried — I felt utterly despairing, depressed and furious with my body for failing me. As a naturopath, trained to believe in the body's ability to heal, that was really bad news.

Eventually, I was so tired of fighting it, I realised it had to be easier to just accept that this is how it was going to be; that I had to make the best of the cards that life had dealt me. And letting go was one of the best things I've done so far. Why? "Because What You Resist Persists!" This saying, coined by Carl Jung, reminds us that the more you resist something, the worse it will get. The converse is that the more you just let things be, the better it will get.

There is a whole school of medicine which believes that repressing emotions can cause real physical pain and health issues. We're not talking about imagined pain here: real, often severe, pain and illnesses including tinnitus, back pain, IBS, repetitive strain injury (RSI), chronic fatigue syndrome (CFS) and over-reactive syndromes like CSS.

Of course, at the start I wasn't really aware of my anger and the depth of it. It was only later on, that I realised how much I was punishing myself and sabotaging any enjoyment in life.

But if you can accept things are as they are — feel the sadness about it, the anger and frustration, the loss, the guilt — then you are not resisting what is going on (even though that may sound counter-intuitive to you). It is better to accept the horrible situation, feel it and stop fighting it. Then you can move on. Letting go and accepting the problem means that you move more easily into a healing state in which you work with your body, not against it.

In the early days of my recovery, a psychotherapist advised me to reconnect with my body by stroking it. She said this would help me listen to my body instead of pushing it away. At home, I attempted to stroke my legs as instructed, but I simply couldn't do it. It felt wrong and I hated the feel of myself — even doing this over clothes — and never even got to the skin itself!

A few months later, I tried The Pear Process (personal enlightenment and release) which involved having to look right into my eyes, in a mirror, as part of talking to the parts of myself that were ill. I did it and had an overwhelming urge to smash my face into the mirror. I felt pure rage which shocked and frightened me so much that I didn't return to it until much later. Then I remembered that I couldn't have my photo taken, or even look at myself in a mirror properly when getting dressed. I had to take baby steps to start accepting myself; you may need to do the same.

Further into my recovery, I promised my subconscious mind that I loved myself, and was going to stop attacking myself and denying myself pleasure. Previously I'd refused foods I loved, not read my beloved fiction books, avoided going out and being with people, wouldn't use lovely stuff on my skin, wouldn't go on holidays. And I justified it all by saying it was because of the reactions. Eventually, I realised that actually it wasn't really the reactions; rather it was mostly avoidance, self-sabotage behaviour and a very deeply hidden hatred of myself. Learning to like myself was vital!

Hopefully that illustrates why forgiving your body is important at this stage! When you're ready to work on this step, we will use techniques like meditation, The Pear Process, EFT and TWR and other tools to allow you to stop fighting yourself, to forgive your body and accept your health as it is. We will also start to build up some compassion for ourselves, and some trust that our bodies will heal and that we will get well again.

Summary

Accepting your illness, your body and your life as they are is fundamental to the healing process. It's time to forgive yourself.

Overview of Step Three: Relax and Enter A Healing State

Our amygdala — our 'stress response' switch, which is the oldest part of our brains — is designed to protect us. Unfortunately, for many of us, this switch gets permanently stuck on. As we saw earlier, when our bodies are hypervigilant, it can result in our systems being overwhelmed with stress chemicals and signals. Rather than keeping us safe, these constant reactions can lead to problems including high inflammation, chronic illness and adrenal fatigue.

It's vital that we learn to calm the amygdala down, so that the body can re-learn how to cope, and can develop resilience. Although all the steps in this programme are important for your recovery, this is arguably the most critical one. We will look at techniques that will calm down your conscious and subconscious minds, so you can start creating the healing state that is central to your rehabilitation.

I learned the hard way how important this step is; I started on the active healing before my system was calm enough to cope with it. It was like trying to train for a marathon with a sprained ankle; while I was doing the right activity for my long-term goal, I was doing it at absolutely the wrong time and making everything worse. When I realised I'd been doing active healing before my body was ready to cope with it, I switched to passive healing: the techniques that we'll cover in this step. I concentrated on just breathing and meditation for a while and it did me the world of good.

Someone once asked me: "If your body is rejecting hard to digest foods, how do you think it is going to cope digesting hard emotions?" Our approach to healing should be similar: I had stripped my diet down to the easiest foods to digest — fish, fruit and veg — and my recovery started in earnest when I did the same with my emotions.

This stage is about that: pure relaxation before we get into the active healing stages, and I'll guide you to find the right relaxing and calming techniques for you and tell you how to use them. These will include:

- Visualisation exercises
- Relaxation meditation and affirmations
- Movement meditation
- Sankalpa (these are resolves/mantras)

Using these tools will help calm your amygdala and parasympathetic nervous system; you'll need those to cope with the later stages of the programme. As I say, I did this the wrong way round so please learn from my mistakes!

Practising various forms of relaxation will also improve your body-mindfulness and start to build a new brain neural pathway for healing.

Summary

Calming techniques might feel gentle, but do not underestimate their strength; they are a vital part of your healing journey. Using relaxation techniques regularly will calm your system down and make it more receptive to the active healing work that's necessary for your recovery.

Overview of Step Four: Use Neuroplasticity Techniques to Change Your Brain

The Pink Elephant in the Room

Whatever you do, don't think about a pink elephant.

Of course, you can't help it; you just pictured one! Your body ignores the "don't" and pictures whatever you tell it, regardless. So, if you constantly think about your illness or a symptom — even if you are trying to be positive about it or even NOT think about it — your body will see just the illness and symptoms. And the more you think: "I'm going to react to this food", "I mustn't think about this pain", etc, the more it will actually happen.

Think of your subconscious mind as being like a small child; it's not that intelligent, but it wants to please and help you. So, if you worry about reacting when you look at a particular food, and keep doing that, the brain eventually builds a neural pathway to make it more convenient for this little thought to take place and starts warning you away from it every time you see it. It's actually trying to be helpful by doing what it thinks is needed to keep you safe.

So, as we discussed in 'What's Causing Our Chronic Illness?', there is a theory that some chronic physical symptoms may have more to do with these Pavlovian-type conditioned behaviours, and brain patterns repeating ad nauseam, than with actual physiology. It can be hard work to change such behaviour, but it is perfectly possible with various neuroplasticity techniques. Your brain has learned to make you fearful, and it can unlearn it too.

Part of this process is becoming aware of what's actually going on in your head and realising what your little voice is saying to you all the time (and I mean, ALL the time). Remember that the more you think something, the more self-fulfilling it becomes; your subconscious is circling on your fear and belief and deepening those grooves in your brain. In neuroplasticity science terms, the phrase they use is: 'neurons that fire together, wire together.' And we're going to consciously use neuroplasticity to change those grooves!

Neuroplasticity played a huge part in my recovery, particularly knowledge therapy. I immersed myself in lots of positive stories of recovery, and it reignited my trust that I could heal. Funnily enough, my partner worried that I was doing far too much reading and fixating on my illness; he was scared I might make myself worse. I saw his point, but as it turned out, it was exactly the right thing to do. The reading was an important part of my therapy and I'll recommend lots of lovely books for you to read too.

Don't confuse neuroplasticity with positive thinking or telling yourself you're getting better. It is not the same thing.

Neuroplasticity takes lots of repetition and application to work, but the results are worth it. Think about stroke victims; they often lose function in a limb, and the therapy is to make them repeat tiny, tiny movements very often in a bid to regain some capacity. Generally, the repeated movements will encourage the growth of new neural pathways in the brain. The old one doesn't go, but it weakens and the new one becomes stronger and stronger, and finally takes over the job.

The more we tell our brains something, the more it changes. And, don't forget: it is when the brain changes that we turn on and off our genes. That is the basis of epigenetics.

The Power of Knowledge Therapy

I read a lot of books during my own healing journey, devouring other people's experiences of illness and their tales of recovery. Little did I know it at the time, but this was a massive key to me getting well. Reading about other people's experiences gave me new techniques to try and clues to follow. Obviously, doing the same as someone else is no guarantee of success and each person will pick up different elements from what they read and watch; we hear what we need to.

One of the most important things about reading other people's recovery stories is developing the trust that you too can get well. I had been completely worn down by my body and I had lost the belief that I might be able to heal myself. I was very frightened, constantly asking myself how I was going to survive if I couldn't eat. As a naturopath, I had always had a very strong belief that my body could heal from anything. I no longer knew how to harness that healing ability and believed that I had lost it.

Listening to others' stories showed me it was still possible to heal; I just had to approach it from an emotional point of view first rather than a biochemical one. If they had done it — some from far worse positions than I was in — then there was hope. And there's hope for you too.

During my knowledge therapy and my own brain neuroplasticity work, I became even more fascinated with the whole field of mind–body medicine. The stories told me that people got better from a meditative, more esoteric route than I expected, not just from nutrition/functional medicine approaches. I began to read more about true psychosomatic illness. Sadly, the term has been degraded to suggest just putting it on, but it is a serious field of medicine and important in non-responsive chronic illness.

Tension Myosotis Syndrome/Mindbody Syndrome

In my reading I came across Tension Myosotis Syndrome (TMS). Dr John Sarno was the first person to describe this condition; it's concerned with how emotions cause pain syndromes and other chronic illnesses. As a mainstream back pain consultant, Dr Sarno became frustrated with the poor results using surgery, steroids, manipulation and the like. Instead, he started focusing on the emotional rather than physical pain. To his great surprise — and mine — this resulted in the physical pain disappearing.

I was so fascinated that I went to see a TMS practitioner for a chat and to see if it fitted my case and she almost laughed at the classic TMS nature of my issues: bone pain as a child, PCOS and severe period pain from teens, IBS, migraine, mouth pain, swelling throat, restless legs, chronic fatigue and hypersensitivity — all common TMS illnesses apparently! It gave me more hope and a different approach and when you're ready I'll show the tools that I used to treat TMS.

Summary

Neuroplasticity will be key to your recovery, and this step will form your brain retraining work and include techniques such as knowledge therapy, STOPs (a technique to quieten your inner critic) and TMS affirmations. Working this step will create new thought patterns and take you further on your healing journey.

Overview of Step 5: Change your environment

In many of the success stories I've read, people found a change of environment helpful. Altering your surroundings and getting out of your comfort zone appears to help break mental patterns and encourage the brain retraining to work.

I took this to the extreme and moved from Warwickshire to Cornwall; I now live right by the sea with the beach a three-minute walk away! It took a lot to do it but, ultimately, it helped tip me into latter-stage healing. I benefited from greater light, increased levels of negative ions around me, slower pace of life, and from getting further away geographically from places I associated with trauma. Don't worry, research shows you can achieve the same result without going to the same lengths as I did. There are plenty of easy changes that you can make, and I'll detail them later.

I was intrigued by my new, instinctive need to live by the sea. I kept having panic attacks when getting into the bath, I couldn't tolerate even reverse osmosis (RO) filtered water from my plumbed-in system, and yet I needed to be near water. It was very odd so, of course, I started researching and that led to some fascinating findings about the importance of our environments in healing chronic illness.

Electricity and water

We are electrical beings; think how your heart pumps, your muscles contract and your nervous system works. And, like all electrical things, we have a positive and a negative charge. But, what if — in some people at least — our electrical charge was upset and was affecting our health and healing potential?

I was intrigued by the work of Dr Gerald Pollack, Professor of Bioengineering at the University of Washington, who studies water in the human cells and tissues, and its relationship with electrical charge. He believes that the water in our cells is not H2O, as we previously thought, and believes it's actually a much more complex crystallised and ordered structure: H3O2.

He believes that we have positive and negatively charged water in our cells, activated by light, which acts like a battery sparking activity and life. Up until now, it's been thought that we were pretty neutral, electrically-speaking, but these findings could throw new light on cellular function. I've included some interesting videos for you to watch, if you'd like to learn more when it's time to work this step.

Why is this important for our health?

Dr Pollack believes that the exclusion zone (EZ) water — as he calls it — sparks activity in the body through electrical charges. He explains that in a cell, we have lots of protein structures — the bits that do the work — and these are positively charged. Surrounding each of those proteins is the crystalline water H3O2, which is negatively charged. Around that, filling the rest of the cell is normal so-called bulk water, which is neutral.

When one of the proteins in a muscle cell needs to contract for example, the EZ water drops its charge and temporarily becomes the same as bulk water. This allows the action potential of the cell to happen: that is, to spark it to do whatever it needs to be doing. Once that action has taken place then the EZ water becomes negative again.

Dr Pollack feels that this has huge health and healing implications. He believes that cells in sick people have less of this structured water in them and therefore less negative charge; this means less activity being sparked in the cells, leading to hypo-function of whatever system those cells are meant to be working for. Ultimately, the more positively-charged the body becomes, the less well it is.

We have known for years that the earth itself is negatively charged, so there is an argument that we should not be any different.

If his theory is correct, then we need to make sure we keep a good healthy amount of negatively-charged EZ water in our cells and — if we are suffering from chronic ill health — we need to take steps specifically to address this (assuming the EZ concentration has lowered). I'll explain your options for achieving this when you're ready for this step.

Grounding

Connecting with the earth is also important. We pull negative electrons from the earth and they have a profound effect on how the body works, affecting mineral levels, oxygenation, immunity and, importantly for us, inflammation and the parasympathetic nervous system. Again, more details and instructions will follow when you're ready for this step.

Summary

Our environment is vital. We need to improve our surroundings and our connection with nature.

Overview of Step Six: Support, Reveal and Deal with the Emotional Side of Your Illness

When my usual ways of healing — which had worked on hundreds of my patients — failed me, I promised myself I would be open to any clues that the Universe wanted to send me, and I wouldn't block them with my existing health knowledge.

Alongside my exhausting illness, I had become terrified of reactions. It's hardly surprising; fear is a real driver of pain. My previous migraine and mouth pain had been excruciating — necessitating morphine meds a couple of times — so, no wonder I was scared of more of the same. Inevitably, things just got worse and worse the more fearful I felt.

At this point, I created a timeline of my life and my illness to help me understand it. Writing this revealed that every time there was a major stress or trauma in my life, I developed a new intolerance or sensitivity condition shortly afterwards, or my existing symptoms worsened. Intrigued, I read up about the links between stress, trauma and illness.

Reading about other people who'd similarly realised the link between their emotional past and their health — and who had got well by working on their issues — turned out to be a vital part of my healing process.

I started to see my symptoms as often having an emotional trigger rather than a physical one. My brain was simply, and misguidedly, trying to protect me and I needed to investigate why it thought I was in danger. That was the start of my emotional work; eventually, I realised that it was my inner child who felt unsafe — not adult me — and that's who my subconscious was protecting. Finally, I could see how my sensitivities were largely a conditioned, learned response and needed neuroplasticity work to change them.

Am I saying there is nothing physically wrong? No, of course not. However, I was suffering so much hypersensitivity and pain — on an extremely restricted diet — that it simply couldn't be my NCGS, Coeliac disease and leaky gut that were causing it. There had to be something else; I just had to work out what.

We've already looked at how ACEs (Adverse Childhood Events) can contribute to chronic illness, and here's a brief recap.

Adverse Childhood Event Disorders and Trauma-Triggered Illness

ACE is an evolving area of medicine that has already found — and is continuing to find — surprising and significant links between major childhood trauma and an ever-widening range of chronic illnesses in later adulthood, including stroke, autoimmune disease, depression, fibromyalgia and heart disease.

This part of my healing journey was a real eye-opener. Obviously, everyone knows on some level that suffering any kind of trauma is not good and is bound to have some effect on a person, but I didn't realise quite how much, nor just how much later in life it might show itself.

Perhaps you don't think you suffered any trauma as a child? Many people — including me, at first — assume that trauma only refers to things like bereavement, violence, physical and sexual abuse. However, the definition is wider than that, also referring to habitual emotional abuse, including bullying, and feeling alone, fearful or unsafe. Obviously, adults can also suffer all these kinds of traumas but when a child suffers it is much more likely to cause a hyperactive amygdala, and that sets us up for chronic illness later in life. Certainly, mine built up over many years and was triggered in my forties: a common time of life for that to happen.

When you're ready to start on this step, I'll show you how to calculate your ACE score and analyse what it indicates.

Separation and abandonment

Similarly, many people who develop chronic illness of some kind have a history of separation anxiety or abandonment. During my life, I've lost four mothers (or mother-figures), four fathers, four siblings, and I was ripped from my childhood home repeatedly and then completely at 10. It doesn't have to be as overt at that, of course. It might be that you feel unsupported by a partner in your illness, or are hiding stuff from colleagues at work, even that you lost your beloved pet or a job. Those are all forms of separation and abandonment, and we'll be looking at ways to restore and improve your sense of connectedness during this step.

Working this step will almost certainly release a lot of long-buried, intense emotions. This can be overwhelming, so it's important to do the work carefully and gradually, and to support yourself with spiritual strengthening exercises, networks of comforting people, and professional help if necessary. As my triggers and beliefs revealed themselves, and were dealt with, I began to get well. I was less hypersensitive, I could eat more foods, my pain decreased, and my symptoms left or reduced. Recovery is so much easier when the fear and pain has left you!

A quick word about spirituality

Deepening your spiritual strength is an important part of this process. However, everyone has different beliefs and feelings. I am not in the least religious so, when I talk about deepening spirituality, I do not mean religion. But I am only sharing my concept of it; your understanding may be different — especially if you are religious — and, of course, that is fine. I am simply telling you what worked for me, so you can adapt as appropriate for you. For me, spirituality was about giving up the fight, accepting and putting my trust in something else: you are free to define the something else however you choose!

Delving deeper into the Universe

Spirituality is our inner-core of strength and, in this step, we will increase it with deeper forms of meditation. I was astounded by the power of it during my own journey — and the emotions it released — especially during one particular patch where I felt heart-sore, heavy-chested and extremely sad. So, I tried a heart meditation to help: Deepak Chopra's 'Soul of Healing meditations' CD. As it turned out, this particular CD was a massive part of my healing process so, when it's time for you to work through this step, I'll explain fully how to use it.

During the sutra, you imagine your heart beating and a point of white light in the heart area. Well, all I could find was a weedy, flickering, pinkish light, and I realised that my heart was really poorly. Strangely enough, I thought of Patrick Swayze lying on the ground — after he's been attacked in the film *Ghost* — not quite believing he was dying! It was really clear; he was fading away and, I felt, so was my heart.

Picturing my heart was so distressing because it looked misshapen, bruised, with lots of weeping wounds. I felt so sorry for it and imagined myself holding it very gently in my hands — cradling it as if it were dying — and I sobbed. After the meditation, and for several days afterwards, I felt very wobbly. But, I was also strangely calmer and more accepting; if that's what my heart had been coping with all these years, no wonder I was ill! I felt I had recognised a problem at a much deeper level inside me, and that realisation and knowledge proved to be very strengthening.

Finally, I started accepting the truth of the emotional triggers of my hypersensitivity illness and turned my attention to learning more about it and doing techniques specifically to help. My experience of that meditation became more and more spiritual as time went on; I imagined myself suddenly rising up and taking a breath — as if I had been under water — then turning into tiny golden pieces. I was part of the Universe, spinning in some kind of vortex of golden light, and it was a beautiful experience. A while after that, a great, big, black balloon inside me popped and I was very depressed for days, feeling hollow, like I was made of nothing. Then, the balloon somehow transformed over days into a transparent column of golden light and became a safe space where I could let go and rant, venting furiously.

After the anger went, I was in a new phase where I felt rather low; I was stuck and staring out at the world. Then I had a sense of the golden light coming out of the tube and hovering like a cloud, eventually going into me like a dose of something. Now, the golden light vortex was inside me and has remained so since then. I think of this as my core of strength and support, and it's very comforting.

This may all sound very weird, but it was actually fascinating to experience, and I understood instinctively that it needed to happen if I was to get well. I accepted what was going on, stopped fighting it and resolved to just meditate.

Meditation helps connect you to the 'Source', which could mean Nature, your God, Qi, the Universe or whatever suits your way of thinking about it. For me, it was a connection to the Universe. I felt like part of a much bigger whole and therefore less alone with the illness and my thoughts. There is no right or wrong way, just what you choose to believe.

Belief is a very powerful thing and can really help your healing if you recognise and use it. These days, instead of thinking of myself as an orphan Annie, I see myself as a 'child of the Universe,' connected to all things. It didn't happen overnight, it sunk in gradually as I repeatedly learned that I was connected to everyone. It feels so much better than being alone with it all.

During my meditations, I started uncovering deeply-buried emotions. I worked through them with various tools, including journaling.

Journaling

This is a terrific way to identify and process emotions and subconscious messages, just bringing them into awareness can be enough to release any hold they have over you. I will talk you through the techniques I used when you're ready to work this step.

What is Your Subconscious Trying to Tell You?

As well as the messages from my journaling, it was helpful to look for meanings in my symptoms. If you remember, the TMS type-theory of illness explains that symptoms are often caused by your subconscious trying to get your attention. Or, they can serve as distractions; there's nothing like physical pain to distract you from emotional pain that's not been processed yet. Often, the subconscious will hold that memory, or event, until it perceives you are stable and finally ready to process it. Perhaps that's why it tends to kick off when we are happy or certainly older: usually late 30s, early 40s. Anyway, I will talk you through how to analyse your symptoms, when you're ready to work this step, to figure out what memories or events are blocking your recovery.

Dealing with What Comes Up

It's hard work releasing these emotional triggers. However, the aim is to raise them out of your subconscious — where they are doing you harm — to deal with them and release their power; not to re-traumatise yourself.

To release the negative charge that an emotional memory or event has, you need to tell the body and mind that the trigger is no longer true or appropriate, you don't need protecting from it anymore, you've moved on, or whatever is appropriate for you. A lot of my negative memories — and perhaps yours — were from childhood; I had to do a huge amount of work on my inner child, and the fractured parts of myself who were still frightened of certain things or holding onto unhelpful beliefs. So, it wasn't the conscious-level, nearly-50-year-old me that had the problem; it was a younger version of myself that needed the help to let go and forgive certain people from my past.

At this stage, I did various visualisation exercises that I'll share with you later. This trauma release work had a massive effect on my physical illness and symptoms overall, and I felt my illness getting smaller and smaller. Still, I was amazed at how many layers there were to my own buried emotions: I'd free a blockage and then be surprised when it returned, until I realised that underneath it was another layer that was now ready to be dealt with. Eventually, when I'd removed enough layers, it felt like I'd reached a layer of trauma that wasn't even originally mine! And, indeed, it appears that trauma may affect later generations from an epigenetic point of view. In other words, the genetic switches affected by the trauma remain on high; this possibly leads to pain, autoimmunity issues and other illnesses, and that these genetic changes could be passed down through the generations.

Physical and Energetic Support

There were many times that this emotional release work would result in actual physical pain or a symptom somewhere, and this convinced me that a lot of what I had been suffering for years must have at least been partially emotion-triggered. Often, I would get tremendous pain in my legs; at one stage my right leg was so sore and tight that I couldn't walk properly or get up the stairs for weeks. Eventually, I asked the leg what it wanted to tell me, and then had a sense of a horrible, huge, black wound on it.

It took a long time to get that healed as it had many layers. In fact, we traced it back to the time I couldn't walk to school because of excruciating bone pain; this was just after Mum had committed suicide and I had gone into care, I'd been split from my home, my sisters, even my cat. Literally, I couldn't stand it. It was indeed a deep emotional wound. To this day, I know if something is really upsetting me, or I'm not looking after myself well as that leg starts to hurt.

Anyway, we have to remember how much trauma and emotion we hold in physical tissues like our muscles. Of course, not everyone will have reactions like this but, if you do, we'll look at some techniques to support yourself.

Summary

This step will teach you how to communicate with your subconscious, to ask it for advice and then use that information to guide your healing. This may sound mad to you, but this is the truth about what worked for me; remember, I'm a biochemist-trained nutritionist and it seemed crazy to me too at first!

Your support network, and developing your inner strength, are critical to this step so we'll also look at how to find appropriate emotional support, how to strengthen these connections and deepen your spirituality. We'll also cover how to physically support yourself during this work.

Overview of Step Seven: Find Out Who You Are Now and Re-join the World

Eventually, hopefully, you will start to feel like all your hard work is paying off and begin to feel much better. This comes on gradually or can be quite a sudden realisation that you no longer feel like an ill person. That means it's time to find a way to step back into the world gently.

Rather unexpectedly, this turned out to be the most difficult period of my own healing journey and also the most difficult section of this plan to write: possibly because I may still be evolving into the post-illness me. For example, just two days ago I had a sudden realisation that I am now a normal person. I have a couple of health issues to deal with in my life still, and am working on them, but what 50-year-old woman doesn't? That doesn't make me an ill person, it makes me normal. I am no longer driven by trying to solve my health problems. Sure, I get down when I have days and weeks when I feel unwell, but I am not defined by it anymore, nor does it dominate my life.

This is so far from the days when I felt I was going to die. I am no longer ruled by fear, fear of the symptoms, of food, of having a restricted, joyless life, of going into hospital and having my needs ignored, of a future full of illness, of getting worse, of losing even more weight, of people getting fed up with me and leaving, of being a burden and dragging people along with me. I'm sure you'll recognise a lot of these, which is why I share them. We've all been there.

Even though I felt so much better, I found this aspect of healing very disorientating and upsetting. I'd spent so long being defined by an illness, moving on from that felt like losing my identity. It was like a great big hole opened up inside me; I felt hollow. While I felt ecstatic that I could eat more again and released from the fear and illness that I hadn't even known had made me, I simultaneously felt sad, full of loss and undefined; it was disconcerting. This may not happen for you at all but, if it does, you hopefully won't be as thrown by it as I was.

A lot of the books in this field suggest that you can't go back to being the same person as you were before. I agree that you fundamentally shift at a very deep level, after this kind of work, and so you are really not the same person as before; certainly, you look at things differently in life and hopefully from a much stronger inner-you standpoint. However, I disagree with the experts who say that you can't go back to your old life.

I missed plenty of things from my old life. I wanted to go to the pub and have a glass of wine like I used to, I wanted to eat in a restaurant, I wanted to keep doing my job the same as before. And I don't think there is anything wrong in that if your life before was a nourishing, positive, supportive one. Maybe they mean if your life was essentially making you ill before, you wouldn't want to go back to that?

Anyway, you don't have to be a crystal-wearing, spiritual yoga maniac after this process — although you can if you want to be! You can go back to doing what you enjoyed and what nourished your soul before; whether that's a glass of wine or going to music festivals to dance, or something else, then that's surely all to the good. All the: "You have changed and won't want to go back to your old life," messages threw me and actually made it harder. If you do want to reclaim your old life, you can!

I was a traumatised child — and therefore adult — so it's no wonder I didn't know who I was after I cleared that from my subconscious. I am definitely quieter and shyer than the over-compensating extrovert I used to be. I used to crave company and now I like my own company. I don't work so hard that I have no time to think any more: a classic distraction technique. Although I am calmer and quieter, I am essentially the same me, just more truthful. It feels like a significant change.

Summary

Essentially, this phase is a coping place, a time of building a much fuller and meaningful, enjoyable life again even within the constraints of any illness you still have. And there will probably still be some constraints because everyone has some; that is normal. And whenever people asked me what I wanted, I always said: "I just want to be normal".

Overview of Step Eight: Investigate and Treat Whatever's Left

We reviewed your nutritional and medication needs at the beginning of your healing journey and you'll need to do it here and at the end as well.

At this point, you'll be able to see more clearly what was emotional in origin, and what has disappeared or improved because of your healing work. You'll be ready to start targeted testing and treatment to deal with whatever is left on a physical level. Some patients even find that they don't need any further treatment at all.

BEFORE YOU READ ANY FURTHER

If this is the first time you've read this book, please go back to the beginning and start reading again. This is an important part of your knowledge therapy! Make notes as you read through this time.

If this is the second — or perhaps third, or fourth, maybe more — time that you've read the book then congratulations on your excellent knowledge therapy work! If you feel ready, then turn the next page and start working through the steps. If you're not quite there yet, not to worry. Go back to the start, read again, and listen to your instinct, it will tell you when it's time to begin work.

7

Working Through the Steps

Now you understand the steps, you're ready to start working through them. I'll show you the tools/techniques/books/CDs and exercises that helped me and other people, at each step, along with instructions on how to find them and do them. It's fine if you want to do your own research and choose different techniques; ultimately, you should always feel free to choose the methods that feel right to you and omit the ones that don't. A vital part of this Healing Plan is learning to trust your instinct!

How to Work Through the Steps

Remember: you should work through this self-help plan with your chosen health professionals.

When you follow this plan, you'll take care of your whole self, and give yourself the best chance of recovery. Note, that you may well find it beneficial to practice more than one step at a time (particularly steps one and two), so move between them as it feels right for you.

Nutritional support (including remedies and meds) is vital throughout your journey of recovery. The two most important times to review your nutritional needs are at the very start and very end of this plan. However, many people make the mistake of fixating only on nutrition and medication, while neglecting the healing that makes up the rest of the steps. Don't fall into that trap otherwise the programme won't work properly.

FINDING the Right Tools and Techniques for You

If you want to explore other techniques, a great starting point is YouTube. Often, I would just search for a specific subject on there, see what came up, and kept exploring from there. Start building lists of your favourite tools, as you find them (Get Pocket and Evernote are really handy for this).

Similarly, I noted all my phrases and affirmations. Then, if I needed some specific help — perhaps for acceptance, or to release sadness or lower head pain or something — I searched through my favoured tools (and phrases) until I found one that really meant something to me. I'd then use that resource repeatedly for a week, or more, or use the chosen phrase in my TWR process.

TAKE YOUR SCORES!

It's a good idea to note your symptoms down and score how you are currently feeling. Trust me, you will never accurately remember later. Noting your score at the start of your journey — and rescoring yourself regularly — is great for showing you how far you've come and to spur you on when you're having a blip. To help with this, you can download the Symptom Checklist we use in clinic to monitor patient progress. (https://purehealthclinic.co.uk)

Finally, remember you'll need to allow yourself plenty of time. This is no small task and you can only go at the pace your body and mind will allow. My advice is it will take at least a year, probably more. That's not to say you won't feel better much earlier than that, but that's enough time for major brain change, the unpicking of unhelpful beliefs, and the calming of the amygdala, to stick. I can't say how long each step will take for you, trust yourself and start to tune in to what you need and what you feel drawn to do. When working this programme, I moved on — or did something else concurrently — whenever I felt like it. I did whatever came to mind and felt important at that point in time. In the end, I learned to talk to my subconscious very clearly and ask it for the next task; and by the end of this journey, you'll be able to do that too.

Ready to start work? I'm rooting for you.

Micki

8

Working Through Step One: Assess Your Immediate Nutritional and Medication Needs

A reminder that — although this step is vital — many people fixate only on this nutrition and medication stage without ever doing the necessary healing work to truly get better. I don't blame them, I was trained to do that and did it myself for years! However, I want to save you from the same mistake. Work all eight steps of the programme, not just this one.

To be clear: **IF YOU CONCENTRATE ON NUTRITION AND MEDS WITHOUT WORKING ON HEALING, THEN THIS PROGRAMME WILL NOT WORK.**

Lecture over, let's get cracking.

Diet

Having worked in this field for a very long time, I have come to the conclusion that most people with unresolving chronic illness most probably have a gluten-related disorder (GRD) or require an autoimmune approach to their diet. I don't really want to say that (because it is encouraging avoidance) but it is actually the truth.

My approach to any chronic illness nowadays is to dovetail the diet and supplement approach in my Gluten Plan (see my website https://purehealthclinic.co.uk) with the mind–body medicine of the Healing Plan. Taking known inflammatory, leaky-gut-inducing foods out of your diet at the start — if necessary — will open the body up to healing and resolve many symptoms whilst you get on with the business of the Healing Plan.

The ideal scenario would be to:

Test for a gluten-related disorder (Cyrex 3), check cross-reactive gluten foods (Cyrex 4) and follow the TrulyGlutenFree (https://purehealthclinic.co.uk/trulyglutenfree/) diet approach, or one of the others such as FODMAP or AIP if you already have an autoimmune disease. All of these are in the Gluten Plan.

Any dietary restriction should be temporary, unless you do have Coeliac Disease or non-coeliac gluten sensitivity (NCGS) on testing. In that case, you should be able to get a lot more foods back in during or after healing, but the grains and cross-reactive foods will need to stay out longer-term.

The idea is to remove any allergens from your diet and foods that are blocking your healing. When you're much better, you can reintroduce those foods to your diet as appropriate. Any diet restriction — if needed and especially over and above the gluten and cross-reactive gluten foods — should be temporary. It's a means to an end, not a life sentence.

Supplements

Next, consider a supportive supplement protocol. For example, in my own case — had I been actually able to take anything — I would have made sure I was on a good TGF-safe nutrient protocol of minerals, vitamins, fatty acids and probiotics: the TGF core protocol in fact. I might have added lots of extra magnesium and potassium for my adrenals and some iron as I have chronically low iron.

The following is the current core TGF (grain and dairy free) protocol which acts usually as a base for making sure you are nourished well throughout the process. Obviously, you can add more onto that if you need to or use different products. Note that manufacturers do change their formulations, so do check on my Gluten Plan on the site ((https://purehealthclinic.co.uk/) for the most up-to-date recommendations.

- ARG MultiViMin with copper and iron
- There are two versions of this multi. This 'with Cu and Fe' version has none of the corn-derived Vitamin C in the 'without Copper and iron' version, so is a much better bet. It does have the more absorbable folate and B12 forms which initially are fermented on corn, but we have found that the vast majority of people have been fine with it. If you are not, use combinations of other vitamin and mineral products from the master list.
- Biotics EFA Sirt Supreme
- Kirkman Pro-Bio Gold Hypoallergenic

You can read much more about the protocol on the TGF website and get yourself the free TGF Supplement Master List and, for even more info, again use the Gluten Plan where I have put tons of protocol ideas and specific supplements for you.

If you're like me and you simply can't take supplements, you use whatever foods you can to nourish yourself. Yasmina Ykelenstam used this approach to get herself well from very severe histamine and mast cell illness. She has written an excellent book (https://healinghistamine.com/the-anti-cookbook/) which might help. Of course, many people won't be able to use many of the foods she includes but pick one or two to boost your anti-histamine (I'm using lotus root tea) or Vitamin C (I'm using cherry juice and hibiscus tea) or lower inflammation (turmeric). Use whatever you need, and gradually, you will be able to tolerate more foods.

If you can tolerate supplements, use the protocols in the Gluten Plan to help you lower histamine, inflammation, heal a leaky gut etc. Do both this and the food approach for faster results and greater support.

Keep supporting yourself like this throughout your healing process. We'll also re-evaluate your needs at the end of the journey.

9

Working Through Step Two: Accept and Forgive

Start by making the decision to ease off — stop fighting, searching, investigating, worrying, planning life in minute detail — as much as you can. I know this is hard, but just make a commitment that you will least be more aware of what you are doing and try to stop fighting your body. Decide to have a rest from it at least for a bit and see how you feel. Although your symptoms probably won't change, you should realise that the fighting wasn't helping you but was simply exhausting you.

You may find you need some help in easing off — it's probably an ingrained habit and stopping something you have been doing for years is tough — and the techniques in this step will help you. Firstly, you'll learn the basics of Transformative Wholistic Reintegration (TWR) and emotional freedom techniques (EFT); you'll use these to practise the acceptance and forgiveness exercises later in this step.

Transformative Wholistic Reintegration (TWR) — previously known as WHEE

This effective and gentle technique was created by Dr Daniel Benor, a specialist in psychology. It worked for me in the early days when nothing else would. It's a hybrid of EFT and Eye Movement Desensitisation and Reprocessing (EMDR), which are emotional release techniques. It takes time to learn but is well worth it; the technique enables you to essentially acknowledge pain and emotions at the conscious level, while talking to your subconscious about the problem.

While it was designed for emotional and trauma release, think of it, for now, anyway, as a symptom relief method; we will use it for its former purpose later in this Healing Plan. (Don't leap ahead, I don't want you to go too fast and make your sensitivity worse.)

In essence, all you do is the so-called butterfly hug where you fold your arms across yourself and alternately tap each arm. Whilst tapping alternately, you talk to yourself about whatever you are trying to deal with.

It is much more gentle than straight EFT, I found. The beauty of it is that you can do it anywhere, discreetly, if you need to, as soon as you feel a symptom or emotion coming on. I tap my tongue behind my teeth, alternating left or right — all over the place: in queues, in the car, even in meetings! I have used it many times to stop a symptom developing. It works most of the time, certainly to some degree or another. This has been my main convincer that emotions and thoughts are involved.

Dr Benor has an excellent introduction to the technique on his website; I recommend that you work through it. Once you've learned this technique, use it to reduce physical pain the next time you find a symptom starting.

You'll find a right way to work this technique for you, in the meantime, you might like to know how I work it. When I feel a symptom beginning, I start tapping with my tongue or hands. I then acknowledge the pain and talk about it. It's important to go into details here: for a headache, I would describe in depth what it actually feels like, how long it's been hurting for, how it makes me feel and anything else that I've noticed about it. Quick phrases won't work here, only detail, and then repetition, are effective. When I've finished describing the symptom in sufficient detail, then I add an affirmation to the end of my previous sentence, for example: "I love and accept myself wholly and completely, I am OK, I am safe."

Finishing with a positive thought — even picturing something that makes me smile — is important. At first, I didn't feel comfortable with the "wholly and completely" phrase, but when I didn't use it, I found the process didn't work as well. Eventually it became second nature.

One round won't be enough, so say the phrases again. Then keep going, being as specific as you can about how the issue makes you feel now, in the past and for the future. Just keep repeating whatever sounds right. Then, it's time to shift the words to release the pain. Here's an example of the words I might use: "Even though I can feel this pain in my head, I choose to let this symptom go now. I choose to release all associated emotions and beliefs, all learned behaviours, conditioned responses, anything and everything that might be causing this or making it worse, I release them all now. I am grateful that my body is showing that something is wrong, and I am dealing with it now. I am looking at the underlying causes of my symptoms and I no longer need these physical messages and signs; thank you anyway. I am safe, I am OK, I am healing."

There are so many ways to do this, so don't get caught up in what to say or how to say. Simply go with whatever feels right for you. It changes for me every time. Just let your mind take over and say whatever comes up; it's your subconscious brain you are talking to here, so let it speak.

Emotional Freedom Techniques (EFT)

Learn all about EFT, and how to do it, from the founder himself, Gary Craig, who gave his technique free to the world. Follow the free tutorial programme at EMoFree.com.

I think the real success behind EFT and similar programmes is the talking to yourself nature of them; it is an excellent way of accessing your subconscious. It's also repeating phrases, so can only help to change neural pathways and ways of thinking — it's neuroplasticity at work. Remember, if your way of thinking changes, so does your brain and so do your genes.

It can be difficult to get started with these techniques. I had tried going straight into EFT, but was having nightmares and symptom reactions, so I had to step back a bit and try the following videos instead.

Self-Talk Videos for TWR

You can get a gentle introduction to TWR (which itself derives partially from EFT) techniques by visiting Bea Resnick's YouTube channel; I used her videos every day for about half an hour. They were a great way into TWR, and they helped to start shifting my mindset.

Tap-Alongs for EFT

In a similar vein to the self-talk videos, tapping along with other people can be much easier than starting to do EFT on your own. In psych-speak, this involves a process called mirroring and is often described as borrowing benefits.

Brad Yates is a popular online EFT coach, based in the US. His website is www.tapwithbrad.com, and he also has a YouTube channel, where you can watch his many healing videos.

David Childerley is a British EFT coach, with a laid-back attitude that I like. He has a popular channel on YouTube, with many tapping videos. He also runs courses from his website, with free tasters available. If you've not done much EFT before — or need a push towards healing and opening up your mind — then I recommend his free '7 Days To Freedom' series of videos. I particularly liked his YouTube 30 day challenges; they gave me something to do every day towards my healing, changing my subconscious and building new neural grooves.

Forgiveness resources

Start forgiving your body by finding a meditation, or resource, that suits you and doing it regularly. I recommend the following:

Personal Enlightenment and Release (The PEAR Process)

This is a powerful forgiveness technique (it's also great for acceptance), and I found it helpful at various stages of my recovery. (I've already talked about my strong reaction to it the first time I tried it; hopefully you will have a more positive experience!) Find out more about The Pear Process on the TMS Wiki; we will explore the TMS Wiki in more detail later in this plan so for now, don't read through the rest of that site until you're advised to.

Brad Yates

Brad Yates has a number of forgiveness videos, if you search his YouTube channel. Try something like 'Beating Yourself Up!' Remember, you don't have to do the tapping, you can use TWR or just use the phrases and repeat them. The point is the self-talk.

Acceptance resources

Work on accepting your body as it is. Try this simple body acceptance exercise: stroke your own skin and repeat a simple affirmation: "This is my body, this is me." Repeat daily.

Also try The Pear Process as mentioned earlier. If this is too much for you (as it was for me at first) then go back to the body acceptance exercise above, and take tiny steps forward, stretching yourself gently to get to the next stage. My therapist asked me to really start looking at my face and into my eyes — when I was brushing my teeth or dressing — and I realised how much I distracted myself from doing it. I made the effort to simply note what I saw rather than to judge in any way. One day, I was able to stare at myself, in a full-length mirror, for 10 minutes. Finally, I realised that I liked what I saw; I looked kind and normal, not hideous and ugly. I truly think that was the first time I actually saw a person I liked staring back at me, even though at another level I had always thought of myself as kind and caring.

Be sure to try EFT and TWR, as these tools will help you with acceptance; see the resources just below too.

For TWR: here's an example of specific phrasing that may help you, and that you can adapt as necessary to suit your own circumstances: "Even though I have this illness — and it has crept up on me over all this time, and I am now fearful for the future — I choose to accept this is where I am now in life. I choose to stop fighting it. I choose to accept it is temporary, not very pleasant, but it will pass, and I will get better."

For EFT: I wanted to highlight David Childerley's very good 'EFT Tapping: Acceptance 30-Day Challenge' on YouTube. There are also several acceptance videos on Brad Yates's YouTube Channel.

Meditation is very helpful, and I recommend Meditation Oasis for their excellent podcasts, two episodes in particular — 'Letting Go' and 'Let It Be' — might help you with acceptance.

As you continue to work this programme, you will be becoming more aware of what's going on in your mind and body. Sometimes this can release some emotions, so the following techniques will also help you find forgiveness and acceptance now, and will help you deal with emotions throughout the whole of this programme. Make sure you use at least one of them every day. You may decide to stick with just one. I used a combination of all of them. Although I changed tools all the time, I always practised one of them every day (even if it was only for 10 minutes). It's all in the repetition and consistency.

Compassion Meditation and Self-Esteem:

A lot of the acceptance work will help you to build up your self-esteem and develop compassion too. Again, David Childerley, Brad Yates and the Meditation Oasis are a rich source of material; I particularly recommend Yates's 'Self-Compassion' video.

Self-Care:

Whilst you're forgiving yourself — we'll come to forgiving others later — also work on your self-care. Perhaps you haven't been looking after yourself very well, I certainly didn't. This might be not taking the time to see doctors or dentists, not being bothered to cook for yourself, even not brushing your teeth as often, or looking after your skin like you used to. It's totally understandable when you loathe your body, have lost faith in it, and wonder why should you take care of it if it's not taking care of you.

Just become aware of it as an indicator of self-hate or anger and start doing at least one thing to better care for yourself. Try and show your body you do care about it, that you are changing the way you think about it and that you are trying to stop attacking yourself. It will listen, and you will start building new neural pathways to that effect.

Here's a TWR on self-care that worked for me. Feel free to use it, adapt as you like or find your own one. Whatever you choose, remember to repeat, repeat, repeat:

"Even though I know I have not been taking care of myself as well as I might — because I have lost faith in this body and hate what it has become — I choose now to start to notice when I am not caring for myself and to change that. I totally understand why I have done this and I forgive myself now. I will work to change the way I feel about my body and encourage it to help me get well. I am sorry my body has suffered so much, and I resolve to feel compassion for it instead of berating it all the time."

Summary

Before we can heal, we have to develop a healing state. Much of that starts with accepting the current situation and making friends with ourselves again, forgiving ourselves and developing more compassion and self-care.

10

Working Through Step Three: Relax and Enter a Healing State

Let's start with a simple activity, from a meditation by Davidji, to ease you into this stage:

What Animal Are You?

Think of an animal that most represents how you feel at the moment. So, why does it feel like you?

Next, think of three positive things about that animal and apply those qualities to yourself.

For example, I saw myself as a deer, a fawn like Bambi, not a great hulking thing with antlers. I had spindly, weak legs. I was jittery, eyes wide, ready to run at any minute. Frankly, I felt thin, weak and fearful.

When I thought about the positive animal attributes, though, I found: "kind, graceful and long-legged" (something that, as a vertically-challenged woman, felt quite nice for a change!) It was a much better way of thinking about myself; I'd much rather feel kind and graceful instead of weak and jittery.

I'm quite a visual person, and I like animals, so I find this exercise rather powerful. In fact, the animal images continued for quite a while and were a good measure of my progress. What animal was I each time I checked in? I shan't tell you (yet!) which animals I went through because I don't want to put images in your head; just trust me that I ended up far stronger and not an animal at all.

Now for calming techniques. I'll talk you through the specific tools, the books, online courses, CDs and DVDs that have worked for me. Feel free to use the exact same ones, or to substitute something similar that you already like. You should feel free to always choose instinctively what feels right for you. Trust your instinct, even if it feels odd, it will be right or there will be a message there for you.

Relaxation meditation and affirmations:

I recommend this 'Yoga Nidra' CD from Sheffield Yoga for ME/CFS. It is designed for people suffering with chronic illnesses such as myalgic encephalomyelitis (ME). Yoga Nidra literally means yogic sleep and is a form of deep relaxation.

Listen to track one, which is a three-minute intro explaining the approach and then do track two — a 20-minute session — every day (once or twice a day, at least) for at least a month or until you feel ready to move on.

Track two is a mixture of three different techniques. I always did it nice and warm in bed or lying down somewhere, usually after work, or when I needed to calm a symptom or emotion. You start by getting comfy, setting an intention using a sankalpa or resolve, then doing progressive relaxation around the body, some counting and then repeating your resolve.

Even if Yoga Nidra is all you do, it will change your sensitivity and healing levels.

You may also like to explore Meditation Oasis. They do excellent meditation podcasts, most of which are free to listen online or download.

Movement Meditation

Some people find they relax even better if they move or exercise. I found doing Yoga Nidra lying down, plus movement meditation was a good combination for me.

Most people would think of yoga as the main movement meditation and that can be wonderful. However, I found that simple walking — while being mindful of what I was seeing, and repeating my core phrase, or listening to something useful — worked fabulously. I went through a ton of podcasts, audio books and success stories, and I'll share my favourites with you in the next step. (However, if you're keen to get listening and reading, then a great place to start is Alex Howard's book, 'Secrets To Recovery' and his online Secrets to Recovery community.)

The other thing I found really helped to release stuck energy and mental/physical tension was Qi Gong: it's meditation for body and mind. I am the most muscle-tight person you could find, and yoga just makes me feel tight and worse. I was probably choosing the wrong type of yoga, of course, but I wanted something really gentle; which is again important for the amygdala for us over-sensitives.

I found two types of Qi Gong that I particularly liked, and I'll tell you about both of them in a moment. It doesn't matter which movement meditation you choose — walking, yoga, Qi Gong or even Tai Chi — just do one regularly. You don't need any specific shoes or clothes, I did it in whatever I happened to have on, even if that was my PJs (which were quite good actually.)

Here are my two favourite types of Qi Gong: one traditional and one modern. Choose whichever one appeals more to you.

'Discover the Ancient Art of Qi Gong'

I followed this DVD first of all and learnt the techniques, responding well to the slowness and precision of the moves. It takes about 15–20 minutes. I found it quite meditative, which was the point, but I also felt better physically. I felt I was really tapping into something traditional, gentle and powerful which could only help my healing.

Once I was able to do it without listening to the instructions, I angled my TV or PC, so I could follow the moves from outside in the garden. I did it barefoot on grass if I could to help ground myself. Eventually, I didn't need the DVD at all and did whatever I remembered or came to me on my own. You're not meant to do loads of it, less is more.

Lee Holden's 'Modern Qi Gong'

Lee has a free introductory 'Qi 101' course available on his website; I started with that and then downloaded his 'Modern Qi Gong' course. I liked this as it gives you simple morning and evening 10 or 20-minute routines to follow. I found it really calming, somehow sometimes more than the traditional version.

I think it was the shaking movements in this that I responded so well to. I've since found out that shaking is a good emotional muscle release technique. It certainly helped, and I missed it when I stopped, I go back regularly and restart it.

We started using TWR and EFT in Step Two and you'll find it useful for relaxation too.

Using the Sankalpa

Sankalpa is a vow: an expression of a heartfelt desire or goal. These statements are an important part of the 'Yoga Nidra' meditation that I mention above; they're also a great tool in their own right. When I started my journey of recovery, I chose: "I will survive", as my phrase. That's how bad I felt, and I had made a choice to get through this and live! Sometimes little phrases just came to me and I accepted them on trust and repeated them. Other times, I chose a very deliberate phrase for something I needed at that point such as: "I release this pain" or "I let go of this illness" or "I ask the Universe to help me." Whatever you feel will help you at any point.

You can change your phrase as often as you like, but do keep one phrase dominant for a while to really set it in. Sometimes, I used the regular phrase ("I will survive" or "I will thrive" or "I am well now") once a day, and then allowed a different phrase to come to me as needed. Sometimes I focused on my physical symptoms ("I let this head pain go now"). I often used the same statement in both yoga nidra sessions, especially when I felt particularly ill.

If you can't think of your own Sankalpa yet, just use the standard healing phrase most people start with: "every day, in every way, I am getting better and better", or just say "I am getting well, I am healing now" or "I am OK, I'm doing OK". It works. Whatever core phrase you choose, start seeing, using and hearing it everywhere.

For example, I used the letters as part of a password on my PC so, every time I had to log into stuff, my mind had to repeat it. I wrote it in big letters on my office door so every time I went in or out, I saw and read it. I repeated it to myself when I was anxious about eating or some other fear, or when I felt poorly. I repeated it when I was walking, cooking, cleaning, doing something mindless.

Movement, combined with phrase repetition, works doubly well and I think is possibly part of how the EMDR trauma/emotional release therapy works, because the eye movement has something to do with helping the brain to change. We'll look at EMDR in more detail later in the programme. This is also why walking whilst repeating your core phrase works.

Summary

I'd recommend that you do both the yoga nidra, and your preferred movement meditation, as often as you can. I often did the Qi Gong after tea and yoga nidra before bed or after lunch, depending on my day. Remember to use techniques from Step Two (like TWR and tapping) to help release any emotional or symptom stuff that comes up.

We're really getting somewhere now and starting to turn your illness around, even if you can't feel it yet. Your subconscious is hearing you and your brain and genes are starting to change. Keep at it.

Next, we need to build the healing state even more and pull away from the damaging one, full of worry and fear. Let's develop some hope and start to truly believe we will get well! This is where the neuroplasticity — changing your neural pathways — really starts to kick in.

11

Working Through Step Four: Use Neuroplasticity Techniques to Change Your Brain

I combined knowledge therapy with techniques like STOPs and TMS affirmations — all in this step — and they made a huge difference to my recovery. The trick with the techniques and reading in this step is repetition, repetition, repetition. And be consistent and thorough with your practising; occasionally dipping into it won't have the effect you want. This work is not an easy, quick fix, but it is eventually incredibly rewarding and worthwhile. Read the books I recommend, and make sure you're reading daily. Combine this with the work we've already done in steps two and three, and the other techniques in this section. Practise and repeat, as frequently as you can.

Knowledge Therapy: Your Reading List for Step Four

I didn't realise it at the time, but the reading I did in this step was a vital part of me getting well. Please do read the following books: I found them extremely helpful and interesting. Learning about other people's experiences and success stories lets us borrow benefits to bolster and encourage our own recovery. Remember that many of these are also available as audiobooks. I really enjoyed listening to them while out walking, or when relaxing.

'Spontaneous Healing', by Dr Andrew Weil, was one of the very first health books I ever bought in my early twenties; I remembered it and reread it in the depths of my illness. It reignited my trust that I could heal, and kick-started a two-year programme of complete immersion in the subject of getting well and mind–body medicine. I heartily recommend you read it.

One of the best books on neuroplasticity is Dr Norman Doidge's 'The Brain That Changes Itself'. Do read it. It brilliantly explores the capabilities of the human brain and how it's possible to rewire and repair it with thought.

I also enjoyed Alex Howard's book, 'Secrets To Recovery'. Howard runs the Optimum Health Clinic in London and dovetails the functional medicine approach with the psychological. His book is a collection of stories of really ill ME/CFS patients — including Alex himself — who all used nutrition and psychological approaches to get well after sometimes spending years in bed. After I read this book, I joined the online Secrets to Recovery site and listened to loads of the stories as part of my therapy. I listened to them when I was cooking tea, cleaning, gardening, walking to the shop, anytime I could.

As mentioned in the overview of this step, I was fascinated by the findings of Dr John Sarno. I highly recommend reading his 'The Mindbody Prescription', which recounts his experience of treating back pain, and 'The Divided Mind: The Epidemic of Mind Body Disorders', which is a lot less about back pain and opens up the field a bit more. It gave me so much hope, I cried! I do hope you will read one of Dr Sarno's books. If you do, you'll see that the prescription for TMS illness is simply to read and read about it until your belief about your illness changes. The prescription is the reading. How cool is that? And that's why I am getting you to do this, of course, as part of your own Healing Plan! Part of the treatment is also repeating TMS affirmations, which helps you recognise that your problem is not physical and helps to turn your brain around; more about this later in this chapter.

Also inspired by Dr Sarno's work: 'Pathways to Pain Relief' by Frances Anderson and Eric Sherman. Anderson and Sherman were formerly two of Dr Sarno's therapists, and they write here about their cases. A lot of back pain, because that's what they specialise in, but inspiring never the less.

Other excellent books that explore the relationship between the mind and illness: 'They Can't Find Anything Wrong: 7 Keys to Understanding, Treating, and Healing Stress Illness' by Dr David Clarke, 'The Great Pain Deception: Faulty Medical Advice Is Making Us Worse' by Steven Ray Ozanich and — a classic in its field — 'The Biology of Belief' by Dr Bruce Lipton.

Reading Dr Joe Dispenza's 'You Are The Placebo' really opened my eyes to the power of the mind to cause and cure illness, and I wholeheartedly recommend this fantastic book to you. Similarly, Dr Bessel van der Kolk's excellent book: 'The Body Keeps the Score: Mind, Brain and Body in the Transformation of Trauma'.

Many people firmly believe that suffering is essential for spiritual growth, however, I've never been able to accept that idea. Happily, I then read Deepak Chopra's 'Reinventing the Body, Resurrecting the Soul' where he explains his belief that suffering is not necessary for spiritual growth at all and that it is our divine right to be happy. More than that, it is our duty to be happy because that then encourages more happiness in the Universe! He focuses on the joy of life, rather than suffering, feeding the soul, and advises us to stop fighting, accept, rest and allow ourselves to be helped. This inspiring book was such an important part of my recovery, so do please read it yourself.

Combining Meditation with Positive Brain-Changing Messages

I realised, at this stage on my own healing journey, that I was responding really well to someone telling me I would get well: whether that was in print, via audio or video. I decided to use that to help myself and went in search of something that would relax me and tell me positive things at the same time. Again, I didn't know it at the time, but this was building on the 'Yoga Nidra' approach of implanting positive healing state messages whilst in a semi-hypnotic state. It was the foreshadow of the hypnotherapy I came to later.

At this point, though, I still felt poorly, in pain and dog-tired much of the time. However, I was feeling more positive and much calmer, more hopeful than I had for a long time. I wanted to do something lying down with someone telling my brain the right things.

That was when I came across Deepak Chopra and Oprah Winfrey's '21-Day Meditation Experience'. I had read some of Deepak's work over the years, so I knew he knew his stuff, but this sounded a bit marketing-hype to me. However, a free one came up, so I joined and had a go.

I can quite honestly say that I consider those 21-day meditation challenges one of the most important things I did to get well. I listened to the freebie, fell in love with Deepak's rich, deep, calming voice and really enjoyed the positive messages and style of it. Do try this challenge for yourself.

Next I bought their 'Perfect Health Meditation Challenge'. I basically needed someone to hold my hand, something that was easy to do, didn't take too long and would get me into the habit of meditating as I was already realising how important it was becoming for calming my amygdala, fear and food reactivity.

They do other free programmes quite regularly and then you can purchase if you want to. Having done loads of them now, I would go straight for Perfect Health; they are all good, but that one was just right for us.

Each day's meditation starts with a little chat from Oprah and then a positive healing type message from Deepak. Listen to this carefully and mindfully is my advice — there are some real brain-changing nuggets in here and a LOT of hope. This is then followed by a centring thought: basically, an affirmation. Then, you do a 10–12-minute meditation where you breathe and silently say the day's 'mantra' or 'saying' in your head. They do tell you what the mantra means in English — they are Sanskrit I believe so mean nowt to me — but the point of repeating unrecognisable (to us at least) words is that if you are focusing on that, you are not focusing on anything else and you can drift into what they call 'the gap', the stillness and silence that is so nourishing for our parasympathetic nervous systems. It takes practice, of course, as does anything worthwhile.

I did the 'Perfect Health' meditation once or twice a day for several months whenever I could, either doing the same day twice or moving on and just repeating the whole programme in a shorter time. I also wrote down the centring thought — or something that resonated with me — on a piece of paper and stuck it on my notice board, repeating it every time I walked past it.

Further meditation

One of the best books about meditation types I have read is 'Secrets of Meditation' by Davidji, who worked with Deepak for years. Davidji explains the various techniques as he goes, giving you little trials to have a go with. He rates mantra meditation (such as the 21-day meditations) and primordial sound meditation as the best. I haven't done primordial sound very much — the most common sound is 'Om', but I do believe that sound meditation is very powerful. In fact, just look at the growing popularity of sound and Gong baths.

Stop and Listen

STOPs is a great technique for becoming aware of your subconscious behaviour and changing it. It's based on mindfulness: once you understand how your amygdala is trying to help you (by reacting to something that isn't actually a danger), you can weaken the old neural pathway and build new, stronger ones to replace it.

All the techniques in this chapter will help your brain learn a new way of thinking; to break that pattern, to allow that neural pathway to start to weaken and to build new, stronger ones to replace it.

The biggest trick for making a change is to first bring a thought or emotion to conscious level. It's really important that you understand that what you think is what is creating your current reality. Ergo: if you want to change to a new reality, a new life situation, a new health state, you have to think something different.

I am absolutely convinced that my own neural connections were so strong, I only had to think something about food and the reaction happened! I have a very powerful mind! But, that's a good thing as it means I can use that power to turn it around.

STOPs

From now, try and catch yourself whenever you think an unhelpful thing related to your condition.

My unhelpful thoughts were things like: "If I eat this, will I react to it?", "What sort of pain am I going to have to cope with today?", "Is this all my life is going to be from now on?", "What happens if the doctor doesn't believe me?". That's a tiny sample. I have hundreds more examples. And hopefully you'll start recognising your own unhelpful thoughts.

For now, choose just one of your most common thoughts and notice whenever you think it. Don't start doing loads, it's too early for that. Just choose one.

When you catch yourself thinking that specific unhelpful thought, don't add to your worry or anxiety by being frustrated or angry about it, just say something like:

"No, I don't need to think like that now" or "that's not true anymore now" or some people simply say "cancel" or "STOP".

Personally, I found saying STOP too stressful. I used humour. I would say to myself:

"Aha, I see what you're doing there, I see you trying to sneak in there, nope, we're OK now, I don't need to think like that or worry about that any more. I'm getting better now and thinking in a new way."

This takes practice and I don't expect you to get this right straight away. At first, you won't always catch it and you may feel frustrated, but I promise that you'll get better at it. As you keep practising, your brain will start listening; it will start to get the message that this is new, maybe I should listen.

Some people find that if they look at something else it can help. So, for me, I would look at a food, worry, say my STOPs phrase and then look at something joyful and happy: the view out of the window, my favourite colour or my cat. I deliberately chose a deep blue turquoise wallpaper for my office, a deep pink one for other rooms, a nice cushion in the lounge, a pretty teapot in the kitchen, effectively having something happy in every room. If I was feeling really anxious, I would go and find my cat and give him a stroke, put my head on his head and let him soothe me.

Do you see how this is working? You are taking one key worry linked to a negative emotion, noticing when it happens, bringing it to conscious mind, giving your brain a different message and linking that message to a positive emotion. All the while, your little child subconscious is learning and that old neural pathway of fear and worry is getting weaker, whilst your TWR, meditation and knowledge therapy is building strong new ones.

So, that's started the work on brain thoughts. What about symptoms and emotions? Let's face it, it's hard to stop a worry when you feel crap, upset or in pain. We delved into this earlier when I told you about using EFT/TWR on emotions, so I am reminding you about it here too.

TMS Affirmations

One part of the TMS treatment is knowledge therapy: affirmations are another important part. You can use the TMS standard affirmations from Dr Sarno's books and the TMS Wiki, see what resonates with you and then continue those and/or write your own and record them.

Here are the affirmations that I used on myself. They are mostly focused on counteracting my fears around food, but they may help you create your own, personal affirmations.

- "My symptoms are due to TMS; there is nothing physically wrong with me."
- "It is only hypo-perfusion that causes the symptoms."
- "TMS is a harmless condition caused by my repressed emotions."
- "TMS is using the symptoms to distract me from the emotions."
- "Since my body is basically normal, there is nothing to fear."
- "Therefore, eating is not dangerous, and I must resume normal eating."
- "I will not be concerned or intimidated by the symptoms."
- "I will shift my attention from the symptoms to the emotional issues."
- "I intend to be in control, not my subconscious mind."
- "I must think psychological at all times, not physical."

I GOT my partner to record Dr Sarno's affirmations — and, later, the ones

I wrote for myself — and listened to them on my headphones when doing other stuff or walking. I combined my TMS affirmations and work with STOPs and TWR/EFT, and it really helped.

After some time, I could actually stop a pain developing or — quite dramatically — stop an excruciating pain, or out-of-control anxiety, purely by using TWR. Not all of the time; nothing stops my migraines. But my mouth pain, anxiety, sadness, anger, panic, swollen oesophagus, breathing problems and painful legs all responded most of the time to some degree or another.

KNITTING A PLAN: Creative Visualisation and Brain Retraining Programmes

Many brain retraining and neuroplasticity techniques have some elements in common, particularly creative visualisation. The brain needs something to follow, to have something to aim at, to know what you want it to build. I thought of it as a bit like a knitting pattern where I had to show my brain a picture of the garment I needed and then make every stitch one by one to produce it.

How does your brain know what your ultimate aim is if you don't tell it? It doesn't. It's only got past thoughts and experiences to go on, so you've got to give it a nice new vision of something to go at. Mine was visualising myself in a favourite Italian restaurant with my partner, holding hands, sharing a meal and a glass of wine like we used to. It's what I most missed: the intimacy of a shared meal out.

Classic brain-training techniques — such as Gupta, Lighting Process, dynamic neural retraining (DNRS) and Silva Method — can help you perform the most effective visualisation, so let's take a moment now to review those programmes and see if they might work for you.

I trialled a number of brain retraining programmes. Rather than go through a whole review of each one, I will give you a brief idea and resources to find out more (however, I will tell you right now that the Silva Method worked best for me). Of course, there are other methods out there and you should always feel free to explore and choose the one that feels right for you.

Dynamic Neural Retraining System (DNRS)

Annie Hopper suffered from severe multiple chemical sensitivity and invented this programme to help herself when she couldn't even live in a house any more. She believed it was a problem with her limbic system in the brain and worked out how to retrain it to believe things were safe for her. It worked. And it continues to work in some pretty severe cases. I'm not suggesting you rush out and get this system, nor that it will work for you like it has for others. However, I was impressed enough to buy it and try it.

I found it did really help, but at the point in time and my journey that I did it, it over-stimulated me as my amygdala was still hyper. It started off my brain retraining focus at least and it did get me through a very difficult Christmas when I was super-sensitive to everything.

There are tons of reviews of this programme on the internet. People say it is cult-like, too prescriptive, just weird… It is certainly a challenge to the established health paradigm, but then I like that kind of thing. You can get a good idea of what the programme is all about from the DNRS video channel on YouTube here and listen to a conference presentation Annie gave in 2014 also on YouTube.

Even if you don't end up doing the DVD programme or boot camp, do listen to the success stories as part of your recovery programme anyway. Many of them are free on that YouTube channel, so get listening!

THE GUPTA PROGRAMME

This UK programme is similar to DNRS, but this time focused specifically on ME/CFS because that's what Ashok Gupta had. I preferred it only because it suited my more UK tendencies (less 'awesomeness'!) and I liked his soft voice and approach. Gupta's is cheaper (or was at the time of writing) and—depending on your location—you might be able to get to London more easily for group sessions rather than having to go to the US or Canada for the DNRS boot camp.

I just did the DNRS and Gupta Programme DVDs and Gupta's webinar series and never went to a physical session. I do think, though, that in these sort of programmes, there is huge benefit in doing group stuff—the so-called 'borrowing benefits' theory I've mentioned previously—means you are likely to get more benefit if you do them with other people rather than on your own.

It can also be helpful to have a couple of one-to-one sessions by phone or Skype to customise the system for you. I found it very hard to come up with the right approach to multiple food sensitivity myself, simply because the programme, at the time I did it, was so focused on MCS and ME.

You can learn more about the Gupta Programme on YouTube and listen to a short introductory video or an hour-long one here (the sound quality's not great, but the info is good). Again, even if you don't do the programme, listen to the success and recovery stories to help bolster your own recovery.

Both of these programmes have very similar approaches. You are basically asked to do certain physical and mental repetitive exercises designed to re-set your learned brain pathways. The approach is based on neuroplasticity and psychology science. I found it exhausting but it gave me something to focus on, and it made me feel I was less of a victim and more in control.

The Silva Method - the Silva Life system

This programme is hugely successful in the US and worldwide, and I was a bit sceptical of the hype around it. However, I found it the best brain-training type programme for me. The Silva Method is basically a set of videos and audios with different specific exercises to train you in their method of visualisation. Their techniques, and the focus on emotion, felt particularly powerful for me.

I did it every day for about two months — I found it really useful. It helped give me my hope back and, importantly, enabled me to build my visualisation muscles: being able to truly link my visual image with strong emotion for long enough to set it. That takes a lot of practice to do it well.

Anyway, do the free Silva trial and see how you feel with it. Be warned, they are heavily into marketing and you do get a ton of emails from them once you've signed up. I found this off-putting but you can opt out later.

Although both DNRS and the Gupta Programme techniques involved creative visualisation, it was only when I followed the Silva Method programme that I learned how to really do it. It is not about simply visualising yourself well, it needs to be done in a specific way, tying an image with a strong emotion. All the brain training programmes I did helped but, for me, this was the real key one. It may be different for you, so do investigate them.

Joe Dispenza's "Mind Over Matter" Programme

After reading Joe Dispenza's fantastic book 'You Are The Placebo' — still one of my favourites of the whole lot — I was desperate to try his 'Mind Over Matter' programme.

I loved his lectures, although they weren't very different from the book, but I found his meditations hard to do, even though I'd already done a lot to build my visualising techniques by then. I felt drained by them —

which probably means they would have worked — but it truly wasn't for me.

If you want to try it for yourself, you can sample and buy his first 'You Are The Placebo' CD on Amazon. However, I'd advise that you don't go for the whole programme until you feel happy with the method first.

Yoga Nidra

We first looked at the wonderful 'Yoga Nidra' CD in Step Three. Track three will help you to build your visualisation muscle; it's quite a simple process, but I found starting with this worked really well and I still do it sometimes today. I did this and then moved onto Silva myself to learn it really well.

Visualisation

My visualisation changed a lot as I went along, but for a long time I kept it the same to really cement it in. It was a video almost — in great detail using all my senses of taste, smell, sight, hearing and touch — of me and my partner in our favourite Italian restaurant sharing food and wine together. I used the colour of the walls and tablecloths, people's voices, sounds of clinking glasses and people having a fun time, looking at each other and smiling, looking at the food, anticipating it, smelling it, tasting it, sharing some, feeling joyful, laughing with the waiter, smiling when a Sambuca arrived and laughing with glee when they lit the coffee bean on the top. Really detailed stuff. It took a good 20 minutes each time!

The trick to it is to link the detail to overwhelming emotion and that's the bit I had to learn how to do — as I say, I found the Silva Method the best one for doing that — although the Dispenza may suit you better. It sounds easy but is not, and you need to do it right. I invariably cried with sheer joy and relief during it: the overwhelming emotion being linked nicely!

Would hypnotherapy be a good way to create your pattern?

I have since wondered if the hypnotherapy that I had later would have helped with this. On balance, it probably would and may shorten your journey to health. BUT, I also think that the work I did to develop my meditative and visualisation skills made the hypnotherapy was much more powerful. On my first session, I told my therapist I had the imagination of a gnat, but as it turned out, she reckoned I was one of the most attuned and imaginative clients she had worked with. I think the Silva Method helped with that by developing a really strong visualisation muscle. She always used to say good visualisation skills made hypnotherapy that much easier with clients so, on balance, I'd still recommend leaving hypnotherapy until later.

Summary

In this step, we've increased the brain-retraining work and become more specific with the messages you're giving yourself. We're weakening negative thought patterns, building healing pathways and, importantly, showing your brain where you want it to go. It's vital to start giving yourself positive messages, specifically that you can get better, that you can trust your body to get well and that you are not alone or even unusual in what is going on.

These positive messages are the core of your brain retraining, of your neuroplasticity work where we are building strong new neural pathways to encourage healing, lower stress at every level and effect epigenetic changes to allow your body to become less reactive and inflamed.

Start with track 3 of your Yoga Nidra CD and then choose one of the more complex methods (like the Silva Method) to really work on your visualisation technique. Then, do it frequently, as well as continuing the other techniques like EFT/TWR and meditation, and using the STOPs technique on unhelpful thoughts, plus TMS affirmations. Remember to immerse yourself in the knowledge therapy as well. If this feels like a full-time job, that's because it is. Your primary job right now is to heal yourself and that takes time and effort — but it will be so worth it in the end!

After working this stage, you should be starting to feel more hopeful, calmer and less like a victim. And, if you're not just yet, that's fine: just keep at your repetitive work and it will come. You are already knitting yourself a new life pattern — stitch by repetitive stitch — for your brain to follow. Every time we do a proper emotion-brain linked creative visualisation then that's another stitch made. It builds up. Now, it's time to look at changing your environment.

12

Working Through Step Five: Change Your Environment

Do you remember how you feel when you enjoy a sunny day, walk on the beach or on grass, how you feel more energised by the sea or in mountain air? Do you feel energised by the wind, or love staring at a real fire? This is likely because, as electrical beings, we respond to negatively-charged environments and exposing ourselves to them is thought to greatly benefit our health at a cellular, healing level. This step is probably the easiest one of this programme, as there are so many ways to reconnect with nature, and with your environment.

Change Your Surroundings

You certainly don't have to move to the seaside, like I did, there are simple changes you can make to your everyday environment in this step. Try some of the following, whilst doing the brain-training/neuroplasticity/meditation techniques, because it helps the brain to shift from the gear it's been stuck in:

- Sleep on the other side of the bed

- Get dressed in a different order
- Take a new route to the shops

And perhaps it's time to look at the home you live in too. Is there a small (or not so small) change you could make to your living space, that would make it a nicer place to be? Even rearranging a room can have a big impact. Initially, I wanted new sofas, and we did change the kitchen and the garden. But then, I realised that what I really craved was open spaces, trees and the sea — and we ended up moving lock, stock and barrel to Cornwall.

Getting grounded

I loved this article on grounding, Earthing: Health Implications of Reconnecting the Human Body to the Earth's Surface Electrons, from the Journal of Environmental and Public Health, and suggest that you read it. The authors conclude that connecting with the earth, *and therefore increasing our negative charge,* may be a profoundly effective strategy to help alleviate stress and many health conditions. And doing this is pretty easy! All of the following increase negative charge:

- Getting out in the sunshine
- Walking on sand
- If you can, make like a kid and bury your legs in the sand!
- Walking barefoot, standing or sitting on your lawn if you have one (if you can do this for 15–30 minutes a day, that's perfect)
- Spending more time near hills or mountains
- Seeking out trees or running water
- Even the little paddling pool, or water feature in your local park or garden might help
- Being outside in windy weather
- You can even mimic this with a hairdryer, to some extent: just think of how your hair goes fluffy or gets static

- Light therapy or a regular sauna
- If you find it difficult to get outside, you may wish to invest in an ioniser to increase negative energy.
- Another way to connect with nature is to eat more raw fruit and vegetables, preferably just picked from your garden or from a pick-your-own farm maybe (the longer off the plant, the lower the negative charge).

The Water Inside Us

I recommend you watch three-minute video (search Gerald Pollack The 4th Phase of Water EU 2013 Off Stage in YouTube) about Dr Gerald Pollack and his work. There's a lot more if you Google. I also found You Tube discussions with Dr Mercola and Daniel Vitalis to be eye-opening.

We've just covered the benefits of grounding above, and the benefits of negative charge. Dr Pollack's theory is that improving the body's negative charge — via any of the activities I've mentioned — builds more EZ water.

Light is also important. Apparently, EZ water is made up of layers and it can build up or reduce. Like plants, light seems to be the main thing that builds up the layers. Sunshine is best, but in fact any source of UV or infrared light (in particular) does it. This all might sound far-fetched, but remember that infrared saunas, laser and other kinds of light therapy seem to help people regain health. Light builds more of the EZ water, which makes our cells more negatively charged, which sparks more activity in the cells and means that there's more energy available.

Note that there are companies that sell EZ water, and filters that will ionise your water, however there is only limited research on these. For now, I recommend that you seek out the natural ways (above) to increase your levels of EZ water.

Having learned about Dr Pollack's work, I started to understand my craving for open space, light and being near the trees and sea. It made me feel a bit less mad and a tad more hopeful that I would heal faster if I put myself in an environment that would increase my negative charge and thereby my cellular activity.

Summary

In this section we've talked about the importance of changing the environment around you to encourage brain changes; how boosting your body's negative charge by increasing your contact with the outside world, grounding and using EZ water will help those changes set. Increasing your negative charge could also increase your cellular healing potential.

13

Working Through Step Six: Support, Reveal and Deal with The Emotional Side of Your Illness

During this step, we'll work on unearthing the trauma and emotions buried deep inside you, and I'll make recommendations for techniques to support you during this process.

LET the Fizz out of the Bottle Slowly!

You'll unearth and release a lot of intense emotions as you work this step. I think of this process like letting the fizz out of a bottle: frequent little releases are better than one great spurt! When I started this work, the fizz release was too much to cope with, so I encourage you to go slowly with this. Take the occasional day — or even week — off if that feels right. You're in no rush, so let your body and mind guide you at the right pace for you. Your instinct is your subconscious talking to you and trying to give advice, so do listen.

Adverse Childhood Experiences (ACE)

First, we're going to look at your childhood trauma and calculate your ACE score as this could be a significant part of your illness trigger and a reason for it not healing. Remember, the definition of trauma is broad, so don't skip this process assuming that you've never had any. As we've previously seen, the higher the ACE score, the more likely you are to have future illness.

Try this questionnaire (https://www.nikigratrix.com/acescore/) and count how many ACEs you have; this will give you an idea of whether your own illness might be partly or even fully caused by emotional trauma or hypersensitivity from genetic changes in your brain.

The score I generally look for is over four, but especially six plus. But even a score as few as two is thought severe enough to trigger illness. My score was eight!

What to Do If Your ACE Score is High

Knowledge therapy is an important part of your recovery, as ever. Niki Gratrix is on a mission to raise awareness of ACEs and you can find an interview she did in June 2016 by search for #159: Create Energy by Healing Trauma with Niki Gratrix. Also, read part one of her 'Healing Emotional Trauma: How Does Our Childhood Biography Become Our Biology?', then follow the link on the page to download part two. I also recommend another article from her excellent site: 'Silent ACEs: The Epidemic of Attachment and Developmental Trauma' - https://www.nikigratrix.com

Have a look at ACEs 101 site - https://acestoohigh.com/aces-101/; it's an overview of everything you need to know about ACEs. Remember, just learning about ACEs, and accepting it may be part of your chronic health problem, will help to change your brain.

I highly recommend Donna Jackson Nakazawa's books: 'The Last Best

Cure' and 'Childhood Disrupted'. The first is a very human story that explains what happened to Donna and how she got over her illness. The second is the science behind it all; they're both fascinating. She also wrote a terrific article for the Huffington Post article that explains ACEs.

Next, a TED talk from the paediatrician Dr Nadine Burke-Harris. Things have moved on a bit since this was recorded in 2014, but it's still an excellent introduction to the subject and an easy watch.

Once you've calculated your ACE score, and followed the knowledge therapy above, you'll be able to accept that there could well be emotional triggers to your pain or illness. The next stage is to strengthen yourself, ready to release and deal with those emotions: I did this process round the wrong way and regretted it!

Later-life Stress and Trauma

While it's essential to examine your Adverse Childhood Experiences, do be aware that stress and trauma suffered in your adult life can have a similarly significant impact on your health. While the ACE questionnaire is obviously aimed at assessing trauma in childhood, you can use it as a guideline to contemplate your adulthood and unpleasant events that you may have suffered. For example: physical violence, financial stresses, bullying at work, homophobia, racism, loss of a parent or partner. Even feeling regularly put down or humiliated is enough. You may have endured more trauma than you first suspected and this may be contributing to your current illness.

Support: Deepening Your Spiritual Strength and Connections

If you're lacking support from family, friends and/or professional carers, then being chronically ill can be particularly lonely. However, there are other sources of support out there.

Groups, forums and social media

Many people go online for support, and it can be wonderful, so do search the internet for a group about your particular health conditions. However, make sure it's supportive. If members are posting lots of negative, worried comments, they could be enabling each other's illness (albeit, of course, unwittingly). The first group I joined was like this and I became quite depressed reading about other people's stories and symptoms, and their lack of success with various treatments. It made me feel hopeless.

When I set up my own Facebook TrulyGlutenFree group, I wanted to avoid that trap. So, members were asked not to moan or whinge, but to keep the focus on positive support, mutual respect, and to offer solutions rather than endlessly go over problems. None of us is perfect, of course, you'll have depressed, off-days, but say what's happened, get some solutions and a hug, then move on. Don't bring yourself and others down.

The mirror neurons theory tells us that the right group support can be vital: seeing success, borrowing benefits from little wins or full recovery stories. So, choose your groups and support very carefully, and if you feel yourself getting dragged down, quit and find another group.

Heart Sutra meditation

I previously wrote about how overwhelming I found the heart sutra at first, but ultimately how healing I found it, and how much emotion it released. Try it for yourself: it's on Deepak Chopra's 'Soul of Healing meditations' CD. It took persistence, but I went from seeing my heart as misshapen, bruised, fading away, to feeling myself filled with golden light. The sutra also helped me accept that my hypersensitivity illness really did have emotional triggers; this knowledge enabled my later healing work. This CD was a god-send (or Universe-send!) for me; I did it every day for a couple of months and I still do it now. It's this one that gave me my bliss moment — level 5 — if you recall from Klinghardt's healing model. Try it daily and see how you get on; it's immensely comforting and healing.

I also credit Chopra's 'Chakra Balancing: Mind, Body & Soul' as being important in my recovery. I hope that you will try both meditations and use them frequently, so that they become part of your healing process too.

What Animal Are You Now?

I've previously mentioned the animal visualisation exercise from Davidji's 'Guided Meditations: Fill What Is Empty; Empty What Is Full' and this is a great time to try the exercise again to see what progress you've made. If you remember, I started off as a frightened deer, all spindly, weak and ready to run. As my healing journey progressed, I became a hare with stronger legs, then a strong muscular snake, and finally a tiny yellow flower with weak roots and reaching for the sun. I wasn't doing any of this consciously; these images came straight from my subconscious and it was a wonderful way of marking my progress. Doing this exercise at various points in the programme showed me that I was indeed going through some kind of strengthening process, which was very comforting and hopeful.

Journaling

Journaling helps you identify and release emotions and subconscious messages, and it's a surprisingly powerful tool. You might find you need some assistance here, either in interpreting the messages that come up, or perhaps there are deep issues that you need to delve into with professional support.

Go and treat yourself to a new pad and pen, so you have something lovely to use each time you journal. Then… how do we journal?

Basic journaling

The simplest way to start journaling is to just start writing. You jot down your thoughts, being careful to end on a happy note. And that's it; you don't re-read the pages once you've written them. Be careful not to drift into self-blame or similar negative thoughts, as you don't want to re-traumatise yourself. Simply write and then let it go.

The TMS method

Remember Dr John Sarno and Mind–Body Syndrome / TMS (Tension Myosotis Syndrome)? Well, there's a complete, free TMS Illness programme to follow and it's excellent. It's based on reading, watching videos, enjoying success stories and lots of journaling. This inspiring course is devised by ordinary people and consultants — mostly from mainstream medicine — who have done it and got well. They've also launched an updated pain programme, which looks like it could be very helpful.

Pennebaker's method

Next, we have 'Expressive Writing: Words That Heal', by James Pennebaker. It's a fabulous book that takes you through a whole variety of different journaling techniques. It's fascinating what comes out when you ask your body in a different way; I couldn't always bring stuff to mind using the TMS Wiki method, however using the other techniques in this book unblocked me and more memories and emotions—which were often quite surprising!—came splurging out.

The Artist's Way

I enjoyed the Morning Pages as described in Julia Cameron's 'The Artist's Way'. The whole programme uses creativity to help get well, so it's particularly good for arty types. You take your journal and pen, then write anything down for three pages without stopping — even if it's just: "I can't think of anything!" — and keep doing it every day. Eventually, your subconscious will start revealing itself. I also recommend Cameron's 'The Artist's Way: Workbook'.

There are loads of other ways of journaling, so—as ever—feel free to go with your instinct and try something else.

Combine Tapping and Journaling

Sometimes I'd journal about an issue, then catch myself repeatedly thinking about it — often getting upset or worried — in the days afterwards. This usually meant it had an emotional charge which needed to be released; anything that keeps cropping up or upsetting you is a likely trigger for your illness in some way.

In these cases, I combined the journaling and TWR/EFT to deal with the negative emotion or belief. I'd read (out loud or silently) the words I'd written and do the tapping to discharge the emotion. I'd often follow that up by chatting to myself about the issue and doing several rounds of TWR until I felt better.

The idea is to release hidden emotions that may be contributing to your illness, and to take the negative charge from them. You won't forget the event that triggered the emotion, but you should be able to get to a position where remembering it doesn't upset you in the same way. My therapist told me that if I saw something on TV that would previously have upset me, and I didn't get distressed or need to look away, then I'd cleared it!

Cognitive or Clinical Hypnotherapy

If you prefer, you can do this work directly with someone, like a psychotherapist, a CBT therapist or a hypnotherapist, who's trained to listen to the words you use and pick out clues as to what might be going on in your subconscious.

My hypnotherapist was skilled at questioning my phrases and uncovering unhelpful beliefs. We then used hypnotherapy to start breaking those beliefs down or changing them in some way, and to change my subconscious behaviour patterns as well as de-charge the emotional residues from my meditations and dreams. You do need both cognitive work (for the beliefs, phrases and the like) and clinical work, but not all hypnotherapists work with both. If you find a therapist who does, great, otherwise consider working with two different therapists either concurrently or at different times.

Here's the process I followed to prepare for the appointments with my hypnotherapist, you may find it useful for your own meetings with a professional:

- In the days before my appointment, I'd meditate.
- After I'd finished meditating, I'd continue lying down and ask the Universe: "What do I need to work on next for my healing?"
- If anything came up from that meditation — either immediately, or over the next few days — I wrote it down.
- I asked my symptoms what they wanted to tell me and wrote that down too.
- I looked up my symptoms for meanings and clues, wrote them down and TWR'd on them.
- I'll show you how to do this yourself in the next section!
- I took my reports to my hypnotherapist for interpretation; she then did coaching, CBT, priming and hypnotherapy with me.
- Afterwards, I'd often suffer with symptoms and feel low. So, I looked after myself, slept a lot, wrote down anything that didn't feel resolved, and reminded myself that there were many layers to my recovery.

- In-between appointments, I TWR'd as necessary and continued with my meditation and brain-retraining work.
- I'd often customise my words to something to help resolve whatever was going on and use a particular meditation that suited the issue. For example, if I was struggling with anger and grief, I'd use a contemplation exercise from Meditation Oasis.
- When I felt ready—and always before my next appointment—I'd begin the process again.

So, we've looked at different ways to bring subconscious issues, stuck emotions, traumas and unhelpful beliefs to the surface ready to be dealt with; you can then use TWR/EFT to control any symptoms that arise as a result, or perhaps find a practitioner to help. Don't forget, you need to calm your amygdala down daily with your meditations too, and these should be deepening. Next, I have a somewhat unusual tip to help you.

Looking for Meanings

While my therapist helped me interpret my dreams, thoughts and visions, and to de-charge and change the associated emotions, I also did a lot of work on my own. In between appointments, I used TWR to control the symptoms and emotions that came up. I journaled and meditated to clear issues, and then took the lingering, deeper matters to my therapy sessions. I also looked for meanings in my symptoms, following the TMS theory that these are hidden issues trying to get your attention. I looked at what symptom types, in which body areas, were supposed to be linked to what kind of emotions and what messages they might be trying to give me. Weird, but fascinating.

So, if I had a pain or symptom somewhere, I'd look it up and use it for clues as to what to TWR, or meditate on. Perhaps it was the placebo effect, but it certainly helped me. There are two main resources that you can use to investigate your symptoms:

META-Health Medicine

This is quite controversial, but it made a lot of sense to me (even if I found it hard to accept it at first). Its practitioners believe that certain organs and body tissues link to specific emotional states and even to specific symptoms and senses.

I first used this to help me with my eczema. In META-Health terms, this is an epidermis (outer layer of the skin) rather than a dermis (inner layer of the skin) problem. The epidermis is linked to the sense of touch, so the belief is that some loss of touch — for example, the loss of a parent, relationship, pet — is the most likely trigger for this type of skin problem (whether the loss happened in the past or present). You then work on this issue using your various techniques like TWR or hypnotherapy. You can read more about the META-Health view of eczema on their website – http://www.metahealthacademy.com/.

If you'd like to investigate your own symptoms, then the best list of organs and emotions that I've found is 'META-Health-Decoding Your Body's Intelligence' by Johannes R Fisslinger.

I went to see one of the main consultants from the UK Meta Health site for a fascinating whole-day immersion. I'm not actually sure what I got from it, other than the confirmation of stuff that I already had worked out (which was helpful in its own right). It was too expensive for me, though, so I resolved to find another way around it, which brought me to a very famous book.

You Can Heal Your Life

Louise Hay's bestseller 'You Can Heal Your Life' includes many symptom meanings and corresponding affirmations. You can either buy that book, and/or do what I do when I have a symptom: look them up on Google! My favourite sites for this are the Alchemy of Healing, which lists all the symptom meanings, and Vital Affirmations. This latter site has the affirmations for each condition, and you say them to yourself to help ease the symptom.

So, when I got a symptom, I looked it up and read about it. And — whether the explanation made sense to me, or not — I TWR'd and meditated on it anyway, just in case! So, do try the same.

Here's another example: one of my common problems is mouth and gum pain. Apparently, this is related to the taking in of new ideas and nourishment, and can indicate a closed mind. So, I talked around that, while doing tapping, in case my subconscious had anything to say! In fact, this was quite telling as my mouth stopped me taking in nourishment, by giving me a sore mouth, it made me not want to eat. I was convinced — that closed mind again — that food was causing the mouth problems and not the other way around. But I repeated my affirmation anyway: "I nourish myself with love."

Of course, you can make anything fit and perhaps I did. But it still helped more often than not, and I was then able to take that meaning to my therapist to work on it further.

Dealing with What Comes Up

Releasing emotional triggers is hard and upsetting work. The best advice I can give you is to expect a rollercoaster and be ready to deal with anything that comes up. It's a vital part of healing; you're releasing the negative charge that a memory has and telling the body that it doesn't need to protect you from it again.

You'll probably find that most of your issues are from childhood, or past events, and you do need to be working with someone skilled in this field who can establish the issues and find which version of you — infant you, teenage you, adult you — has each issue.

I needed to do a lot of forgiveness work, and I talked to many people (in my head, not in person) that I needed to forgive, during my hypnotherapy sessions. In the latter stages, I had mini-me hand-in-hand — again, all in my head, of course — in my normal life. One of my favourite techniques came from one of my early hypnotherapy sessions and I share it for you; perhaps you'll want to try it yourself.

My therapist asked me to visualise a pain or symptom and, when I did this, it often took some shape or form. Occasionally it was even someone I knew. Furthermore, I invented a whole team of ninjas inside my body who were always there to support me. They did the physical work around my body — such as calming pain or turning down my fear — and sometimes wore hard hats, or had clipboards, or other variations depending on their job. I'd visualise the ninjas, with me, on the top of a big mountain in a safe circle and we would invite the form to come and talk to us and tell us what the problem was. Sometimes I had to repeat the exercise several times but, eventually, the form would stop coming, and that emotion, memory or symptom would disappear or ease as the issue resolved itself.

This work takes quite a while, so do be patient and trust that it's working for you. Expect symptoms to come up after sessions and use your TWR/EFT, meditation and brain-retraining techniques to deal with them; they are temporary and part of the process. After the sessions, I'd often experience something — perhaps feeling hyper, experiencing pain, hearing loss, migraine, an emotional meltdown — and I'd often go straight to bed and sleep for England!

Let it all process and clear through. Write everything down so you can go back and report and work on anything residual. Working in this way means that you're always moving forwards: step-by-step, little by little. Some people need loads of sessions, some need only a few to release what's trapped. As ever, trust your instinct to see what's right for you.

Gradually, you will find you need fewer sessions — or certainly longer between them — and you should feel you are getting into a real healing state and your physical, mental and emotional state will start improving.

Do be aware too, though, that you may feel more anxious or low during this process as your true self is revealed, but we'll talk more about this in the next step.

Physical and Energetic Support

The emotional release work often results in actual physical pain and/or symptoms; if you react like this then the following techniques will help you support yourself.

Energy-Clearing or Balancing Techniques

When we have hypnotherapy — or any form of emotional clearance — it brings things to the surface and can affect our energy patterns. I certainly felt out of whack at times as I went along: sometimes too much hyper energy, often too flat. Looking back, I wish I'd had an energy-balancing treatment, like reiki or acupuncture, after sessions.

Reiki

When I got my first-ever migraine, it simply wouldn't go. After a couple of weeks, even beta blockers hadn't touched it and I was at my wit's end, so I tried reiki. I realise now that the migraine coincided with a major life shift, having ended one relationship and started a new one, and I was holding a lot of tension. Indeed, during the session, I felt a huge blackness move through me, from my feet and up my body. It felt awful and I burst into tears and sobbed for ages. The poor practitioner was a little alarmed. But, the migraine went, and I didn't have another one for years. Anyway, I recommend you try some sort of reiki: perhaps distance reiki if you can't easily get to a practitioner.

Bowen technique

I did have some Bowen sessions later in my recovery. It's a combination of muscle release and energy-balancing — my partner used to be a practitioner, so I knew the value of it — and I thought it would be a good one for me. Most people find that, after the first few sessions, they feel like they've been hit by a train, and then the body comes into better balance and calms down.

However, I was still feeling like I'd been hit by a train after my fifth session. This was at the time where I'd started feeling better and was able to tolerate more foods so — although the Bowen was definitely working and stopped several symptoms — I couldn't cope with feeling completely fatigued for days afterwards and decided to give it up. It's a shame that I couldn't continue the sessions, particularly as Bowen puts a lot of emphasis on the jaw and my main symptoms were mouth and jaw pain. You may have a better experience with Bowen than I did.

Muscle-Release Techniques

We've already covered Qi Gong. The shaking in it is known to release muscle tightness and stuck energy. Hopefully it's already part of your healing routine, if not, then now's the time to give it a go.

TRE (depending on who you ask, it stands for Tension and Trauma Releasing Exercises, Tension/Stress Release Exercises, or Total Release Experience) is another form of muscle release exercise. It involves involuntary shaking, much as you see animals in nature do it when they are stressed, but in a much more intense way than the Qi Gong. I've not tried it personally, but that's only because there doesn't seem to be a practitioner who's local to me. However, knowing how I hold tension and emotion in my muscles, I'm sure that it would help. You can find more about it here (http://treuk.com/who-is-tre-for/), and watch an excellent, introductory video about it on You Tube.

Somatic Experiencing is another therapy along the same lines, and Dr Peter Levine talks about it in another You Tube video.

Psoas muscle

I suspect that all muscle-releasing techniques have a lot to do with releasing the psoas muscle (essentially, it's the muscle that joins the upper body to the lower body). When I trained as a massage and manipulative therapist, we were warned to watch for emotional releases when working on the psoas. You can find any number of psoas release exercises on YouTube. Even certain yoga poses can do it, and there is a simple You Tube video you can watch. I find it very comforting and sometimes do it instead of meditation, or when I am listening to success stories and podcasts. If you're new to yoga, you may wish to have a few starter sessions with an expert who can teach you some home exercises too.

Massage

As an ex-massage therapist, I would be remiss not to mention massage as a tool to release tension in your muscles or mind. But, do get the right kind. There are basically two main types of massage: relaxation and remedial.

Relaxation Massage

In a chronic illness recovery programme, you need relaxation, not something that stimulates or causes muscular pain or tenderness afterwards. So, you could choose an aromatherapy massage, or a plain oil massage if you are sensitive to essential oils or strong smells. I have been known to take my own grapeseed oil in and ask the therapist to use it; any good one will be happy to do so.

Relaxation massage is light-touch and soothing; the therapist should be using slow, long strokes across the muscles with enough pressure to feel it's doing something, but not forcing the lymph around as a remedial massage therapist might. You can see any number of aromatherapists and masseurs locally, but, sad to say, they can be a bit hit and miss. If you find a good one, then stick with them, they're worth their weight in gold. Try to get a recommendation or at least choose someone trained at a good school (although, bear in mind that this doesn't actually guarantee they are good). I firmly believe that anyone can massage but, with some, it's an art form and the care applied to the touch confers the most benefit. I loved doing it, and it is intensely relaxing for the massage therapist too if done well.

I'm a bit out of touch with the massage scene now, but you won't go far wrong with anyone trained by either Shirley or Penny Price. In fact, I was trained by Shirley and did my final, nerve-wracking, exam massage on her daughter. Penny, who now runs the training academy (https://penny-price.com/) and has a therapist directory.

Remedial Massage

Just in case you do end up needing remedial massage, find a therapist who's associated with the National Association of Massage and Manipulative Therapists, NAMMT.

Other Modalities

Of course, there are many other different physical modalities to choose from. You might prefer anything from the many Myofascial Release techniques, to craniosacral therapy, to Polarity Therapy, to Zero Balancing or BodyTalk. Again, choose the techniques that call to you and feel right to you. Personally, I would favour a modality that mixes the physical and energetic as they are so intertwined.

Reminder: if you get any symptoms from this work, don't be thrown. They're only temporary. Of course, that's said with hindsight; some of mine lasted for so long I started to worry they were genuinely pathological problems. The trick is not to panic, not to traumatise yourself. Accept it as a process — albeit not a pleasant one — but a process none the less. Talk to your therapist about anything that worries you but do stick with it, remembering that you might need to dial back a bit, rest, regroup and try something more gentle. Our job is to support and encourage a healing state, so be kind to your body.

Summary

We've done a huge amount of vital work in this step: learning to talk to the subconscious mind, listening to any messages, and then releasing the issues that arise. This takes time, self-kindness and support (preferably using a good therapist). Rome wasn't built in a day, and you won't be rebuilt in one either.

Think about your support networks and systems. Drop any negative ones — they won't help you change your brain pathways — and find new, positive ones to benefit from the mirror neuron theory. Do be sure to continue your meditation, brain retraining and knowledge therapy whilst you're doing the release work, this will keep building your inner strength and resilience.

Remember to write down any visions, feelings, dreams or nightmares if they crop up: these are messages from the subconscious for you to work with so listen to them. Use your TWR/EFT/tapping techniques to lower any emotional and physical responses and look for a support person to help you process anything that comes up that you can't clear.

14

Working Through Step Seven: Find Out Who You Are Now and Re-join the World

In this stage, you have to get back out there in some way, to take bits of your pre-illness self and the post-illness self to define a new *you*. Many people change careers, relationships, get some life coaching and think very seriously about what they want to do with this new post-acute illness phase. This thinking and reviewing stage was very disorientating; I made wrong career decisions, felt very unsure of myself, tried volunteer jobs, new locations, new ways of working, got back in touch with people, tried to make new friends, all in a bid to find myself. It is only really by doing those things that I worked out what I wanted to do next and who I wanted to be.

You may find that you need to go through a similar process. As you do, trust and honour your instinct, thinking: 'that felt right', or 'no, that's not me', and adjusting accordingly.

Are you ready for this step?

Earlier, we looked at Patricia Fennell's four phase model; Step Four is "Learn to integrate your suffering in a new life." The illness might be there, but it's only a small part of you and doesn't define you anymore. Concentrating on this final reintegration phase is very useful at this point in the healing path.

Fennell, in her excellent 'The Chronic Illness Workbook' gives a few clues so you can recognise more easily when you are in the reintegration phase. See if you can relate to these:

- You understand that recovery, stabilisation and relapse are all part of the normal cycle of illness, and don't let moving between these stages faze you. You recognise the phases of illness and can help yourself, or ask for help when you need it.
- You incorporate the aspects of your pre-crisis self that you want to keep, and integrate them into your post-crisis self, to define a new you.
- You build and enjoy social relationships around the reality of your illness and make no apology for any disability or special needs. It's just you, take it or leave it.
- Your focus goes from you being on your own in the universe, to including the world at large, you don't need so much inner focus.
- On good days, you work with your illness and lead a fuller life. On bad days, you hang onto the fact that you know how to work towards better days, and that they will come. (One of my favourite mantras, to use with TWR or brain retraining is: 'this is temporary, it will pass.')

If you recognise these, then you're probably ready to start working this step. If you don't feel ready then remember that there is no rush (but do check with your practitioners, as they may feel that you need to push yourself a little.) You can keep working the earlier steps of the plan until you are primed for this stage.

Reading and Workbook Therapy

Read at least one — and as many as you'd like — of the following books:

I mentioned Patricia Fennell's Phase Four explanation in the overview of this step, and I highly recommend that you read her 'The Chronic Illness Workbook'.

Michele Rosenthal has written three great books on healing and moving on from Post-Traumatic Stress Disorder. The most recent one — 'Heal Your PTSD' — is a good place to start as it summarises everything. Her other books are 'Before The World Intruded' (about how she started to realise PTSD was a big part of her issues) and 'Your Life After Trauma' (which is a workbook about recovering and creating a post-trauma identity), and I found them a useful part of my reading therapy. Michele also recommends a book by Glenn Schiraldi: 'The PTSD Sourcebook'.

Pete Walker's book 'Complex PTSD: From Surviving to Thriving' has some useful chapters on recovery and identity, especially the section on recovery signs. Seeing some of them in myself helped me realise in my conscious mind that I was indeed in recovery.

Learning from Other People

I always find reading others stories of how they recovered after illness helpful, and I liked this blog post about illness, and the associated loss of identity - The Long And Winding Road on the PermanentWellness blog. In the comments, a poster quotes the Chinese philosopher Lao Tzu, from his book 'Tao Te Ching':

"Do you have the patience to wait

Till your mud settles and the water is clear?

Can you remain unmoving

Till the right action arises by itself?"

It's a beautiful thought, and one that is particularly pertinent to this step.

Do read this 'The loss of 'self' in chronic illness is what really hurts' blog post on https://myheartsisters.org/ – based on the work of US sociologist Kathy Charmaz. It really resonated with me. The author goes through the loss of self, as it happens step-by-step in chronic illness, and bemoans the fact that mainstream thinking doesn't include the loss of self as part of the suffering. It seems we have to go through the loss of who we were and suffer that until, later on, we find a new self. It's a painful process. Be sure to scroll down and read the comments, as there is much to relate to there as well.

I listened to lots of podcasts, watched videos and read or listened to books and posts on reintegration when I was feeling lost (again, a lot of this material came via Secrets to Recovery site). I found it helped me to see what was going on and why I was feeling out of it — the knowledge therapy at work again. There's also a wonderful resources section on Michele Rosenthal's 'Heal My PTSD' site.

Handling Bad Days, Weeks, Months…

Patricia Fennell believes that many people with chronic illness will never get to a zero percent illness level; that we will all be dealing with one thing or another on an ongoing basis and will probably need coping strategies. (We must remember here that she is talking about unremitting chronic illness like MS or post-cancer, whereas I am hoping we are mostly able to get ourselves physically much better and won't have to cope with so many illness constraints.) We will also have stresses and strains as everyone does in life and those events that will probably tip us back into acute Phase One for a while; the crucial difference is that we recognise it this time and know the strategies to turn it back around much faster than we did before.

Indeed, my own path to health hasn't been smooth — when is it? When I wrote the bulk of this plan, I was doing really well. I had managed to start getting a lot of foods back in and most symptoms had gone or calmed somewhat. I was at a stage where I was feeling pretty normal most of the time and — having been limited to a restricted diet before — was eating like a King! Finally, I was able to enjoy fish, dark chocolate, wine, beef, eggs, nuts and other foods that I'd sorely missed. As the nutrients started to go back in from a more expanded diet, I felt loads more energy. My restless legs went completely, I didn't suffer from hay fever — for the first time since my teens — and I stopped reacting to smells. Furthermore, I didn't have a full-on migraine for over 4 months. Bliss!

I finally felt able to plan things again and start setting up some new work. I was re-entering the world at last, and doing it in a fun, positive way.

And then I was hit by several stressful events in quick succession. This overwhelmed my resilience and my physical health tipped backwards — neatly illustrating the effect emotions and psychology can have on our physical symptoms and the fact that sensitive people are always vulnerable to it. Hence the need always to keep life calm. This is a classic Fennell Integration Stage 4 picture — our health can still go up and down in this phase, much to our annoyance.

I started getting incredible pain in my right-hand jaw joint (I supposed it was all that teeth clenching); it necessitated between 10–16 ibuprofen a day, for over two months, plus steroids. I eventually worked out that the jaw pain had been started by mainly inflammatory foods that I was OK with before: eggs, meat, coffee, wine, chocolate. This is testament to the effectiveness of the brain retraining because I never considered food as the cause until much later, whereas before it would have been my first thought.

Essentially, my gut had become leaky again — the gut–brain axis at play

— the stress had caused a gut sensitivity issue again, and the ibuprofen had compounded it.

So, I'm currently back on the healing path, working through the previous steps in exactly the same way I've told you to do. It's different this time as there is a lot less emotional release required, it is more about reminding my amygdala I am still safe, calming it down, building my resilience and focusing on re-healing the leaky gut. It's a much easier journey this time, and I'm confident that I'll get that wine and chocolate back, I just have to keep following the appropriate elements of the path.

Learning from Yourself

I believe that creating a new identity comes from getting out there, and doing stuff, and seeing what fits you now and what doesn't. Do you like reading the same books, going to the same places, even wearing the same clothes as before? I wanted to grow my hair longer and wear looser clothes; is that just getting older or was I becoming a hippy-chick since I'd moved to Cornwall?

The new you will evolve and emerge over time, you don't really have to do anything, it will happen as and when it is meant to, and you are ready for it.

Summary

In this section, we've discussed how to start reintegrating with the world at large a bit more. Are you ready for that? How will you know and who are you going to re-enter as? Are your boundaries ready to be tested?

Physically, by this point, many of your original symptoms and conditions will probably have resolved themselves because they were emotional or traumatic in origin. But what about anything that's left? Time to focus on that in our final step.

15

Working Through Step Eight: Investigate and Treat Whatever's Left

Time to review your nutritional and medication needs again: follow the instructions in 'Working Through Step One' to choose the appropriate supplements.

After the core healing work…

When you get to the point where you are reintroducing foods, feeling like a normal person again and are reintegrating back into the world as a non-ill or partially-ill-but-it-doesn't-matter-as-much-anymore-person, that's the time to start looking at your physical side again, at the biochemistry and thinking: What is still happening? Could any of this be biochemical or nutritional in origin?

When I first worked through this step, the things I was left with were migraines and mouth sores. They were miles better and less frequent than they had been, so some of it was clearly emotional in origin. Of course, my own healing journey is still continuing, and I'm sure that more emotional stuff will come up when its ready. Do keep alert to that.

So, at this stage, you'll need to analyse your symptoms. Here's an example of how I've previously examined my migraines: I'd start by thinking: 'Maybe it's a chronic magnesium deficiency?' And I'd keep analysing from there. If I had been able to take the magnesium at the start, the migraines may have got better more quickly, but at least I can take it now. A red blood cell magnesium test shows that my levels are on the floor, so I take a magnesium spray. Unfortunately, I forget to go slowly with substances that my body hasn't seen in years, I take too much and get dizzy. I remember to do a hair test to check the balance of my electrolytes. Results show that my potassium looks low, so I confirm with a potassium test. Presumably the magnesium had pushed my potassium levels down. So, I stop magnesium and instead add coconut water — a new food — into my smoothies for a month. After a month, I restart the magnesium at lower dose. My migraines are improving.

Similarly, let's try the same exercise with my mouth sores. Could this be a lack of zinc, needed for healing of the mucous membranes? Again, had I been able to take the zinc carnosine in the leaky gut protocol, perhaps this would have healed better. I check my zinc status; it's very low. So, I start taking zinc and probiotics, made into a paste with turmeric, to strengthen the membranes and lower inflammation.

Do you see where I am going with this?

What are you left with? What could be wrong biochemically?

It may well turn out that my migraines are partly hormonal as I enter perimenopause. Perhaps part of the issue is neurological damage from the gluten? It might be my low iron status. It could be that toxicity overwhelms my liver and triggers an overload migraine. I am very much suspecting this last one as my migraines are triggered by chemical smells (but only if I've had another exposure, or toxin, like coffee or alcohol). It could be all of the above. Most chronic symptoms are chronic because they are not simple; they are usually multi-layered.

So, in this case, I should check my hepatic detox capacity. Can my liver cope with chemicals? What is my methylation status? Am I genetically weak at breaking stuff down?

Here you can see that I'm targeting my two remaining symptoms and working them out, and that there are several factors to check and target with each. Can you imagine what that would be like when you have ten or fifteen symptoms or conditions? This is precisely why I recommend you leave this investigative stuff until you can see what you're left with after the main healing stage. Most people never get to the end of it as it is simply too complex and multi-factorial. They never really get well because it is too complex to unravel. Simplifying it really matters.

Today, I am focusing on my leaky gut (triggered by stress, as I explained in Step Seven) and trying to figure out if there are other biochemical reasons why my gut won't stay healed. As I explained, when you recover from chronic illness, you do move up and down the various models. Healing isn't linear, and I'm living proof of that. However, all you need to do is work through the appropriate steps of this programme again to deal with that (so I'm also working to improve my physical resilience to stress, using those earlier steps). Even if you suffer a major setback, you'll be much better equipped to continue your healing work.

I was delighted to notice that, when I faced setbacks in my health, I never went back to square one; my energy, cognitive and emotional health held up, plus I only had to eliminate a few inflammatory foods instead of going back to a massively restricted diet. Even better, I still feel like myself, instead of losing my identity to ill-health again. It's so important to recognise the progress that we've made, so now's a great time to fill out the Symptom Checklist again. Compare it to your original answers and see how far you've come.

Remember to look after your amygdala so that it always remains nice and calm; I recommend that you keep practising meditation and Qi Gong — or whichever techniques work for you — and make it a life-long habit.

SUMMARY

You need to support yourself, throughout this programme, with nutrition and functional medicine. Analysing the symptoms that you're left with after the main healing work has finished is much easier: you'll be working on a less confused and complex picture. Indeed, some people find that they don't need any treatment at all in this final stage. And remember that healing isn't linear, although this is the final stage of this plan, you may need to revisit earlier steps if further issues arise and need clearing. All you have to do is listen to your body, respond accordingly, and keep following the healing path towards better health.

16

Summarising Your Journey

You now have all the tools and tips that I used for my own recovery, and hopefully you're on your way to good health too.

Throughout this plan, we've been thinking about chronic, unresolving illnesses in a different way: taking in emotional triggers, Pavlovian neural pathways, unhelpful beliefs and, possibly, trauma. Our job has been to go with that premise, investigate it for ourselves and then follow the eight steps to healing. We release emotional triggers, calm the amygdala system, change the subconscious and conscious minds simultaneously, and develop stronger, more helpful neural pathways using neuroplasticity techniques. Finally, we develop a new identity and enter the world again as a well person. Through all that, we support ourselves nutritionally and, at the end, deal with anything on a physical level that is still left.

This isn't an easy process, but it's worth it, I promise! You should come out of this process stronger on every level, having left your fear drivers behind. You'll be much more in control of your body, your mind, your emotions and your life. Furthermore, you should come out of it feeling normal — which is what most of us just want — having a normal life, doing normal things, going to normal places, eating normal foods. Well, you can. Have a go at the eight steps, and I look forward to hearing from the normal you in due course.

Repeat with me: "I will get better, I will have a normal life and do normal things again and the process has already started. I am getting better already. This illness is temporary, it will pass and something inside me is already changing."

I wish you good luck, and good health, on your healing journey.

Micki Rose

17

HEALING PLAN GLOSSARY

ADVERSE CHILDHOOD EVENTS - ACEs

Adverse Childhood Events (ACEs) are known to impact on future health. The term comes from the US Centers of Disease Control and Prevention (CDC) Kaiser Permanente Adverse Childhood Experiences study, conducted in the 1990s, one of the largest investigations of childhood adversity and later-life wellbeing.

Researchers found that childhood trauma and adversity can lead to the onset of chronic physical, mental, emotional and sociological problems in later life. It is thought that the events harm children's developing brains and change gene expression. This can profoundly affect their ability to cope with stress, and can damage their immune systems resulting in illnesses that show up decades later. There have been hundreds of confirmatory and expanded studies and research papers published since. There is also a recognition that later-life adverse events can have a major effect too.

People complete a specific questionnaire to determine an ACE score. See the questionnaire here.

THE AUTOIMMUNE PROTOCOL - AIP

The Autoimmune Protocol (AIP) has evolved mainly in the US as an approach for people who have autoimmune diseases. It is a step on from TrulyGlutenFree in that people avoid not only the grains, dairy and cross-reactive gluten foods, but also many inflammatory and common allergenic foods such as legumes, nuts, seeds and eggs. The purpose is to lower the inflammatory reaction in the body and remove autoimmune food triggers with the aim of reducing or reversing the autoimmune condition. I have written much more about this in my https://www.ecwid.com/store/purehealthshop/TrulyGlutenFree.

DYNAMIC NEURAL RETRAINING SYSTEM - DNRS

Created by Annie Hopper, herself a severe multiple-sensitivity sufferer in the US, the Dynamic Neural Retraining System is an approach using neuroplasticity and amygdala-calming techniques similar to the Gupta Programme. It help conditions such as chronic fatigue and hypersensitivity.

It is run as an in-person programme or distance learning using DVDs and coaching. https://retrainingthebrain.com/

EMOTIONAL FREEDOM TECHNIQUE - EFT

The Emotional Freedom Technique, founded by Gary Craig and given free to the medical world, is a non-invasive version of acupuncture. Tapping with the fingertips is used instead of needles.

Often simply called 'Tapping,' the technique is used to help release the emotional causes and triggers of physical and mental illness, but can also help reduce physical symptoms. Based on the Eastern medicine theory of energy meridians, tapping on certain points of the head, face and upper body in a specific order along those meridians, whilst talking through the issue being worked on, is thought to help clear stuck emotions which could be contributing to illness and preventing the body from healing.

The verbalising part of the therapy incorporates elements of neurolinguistic programming (NLP), neuroplasticity and cognitive behavioural therapy (CBT), helping people come to terms with memories and events and build new, more helpful neural pathways.

There has been much research into EFT showing clinical effectiveness for many issues including pain, trauma and anxiety. One way it is thought to help is that tapping the acu-points sends a signal to the limbic system, specifically to the hippocampus and amygdala, both of which date-stamp our memories and monitor danger levels, suggesting to them that the issue is in the past and that we are safe now.

EFT can often provide substantial relief and is used most often as a self-help therapy. However if you have long-lasting or intense emotional or physical trauma, please work with your chosen health practitioner. https://emofree.com/

EXCLUSION ZONE WATER - EZ WATER

Dr Gerald Pollack coined this term, which means Exclusion Zone water. His research suggests that we have a kind of living water, with a different structure to normal H2O, in our cells and extracellular tissues. This H3O2 water is more dense and alkaline, is affected significantly by light and has a negative charge, holding and delivering energy like a battery. It is called exclusion zone, because one of its properties seems to be the exclude molecules (i.e. toxins) from the cells.

It was previously believed that water came in only three states: as water, vapour, or ice, but many researchers are working on this fourth state of water, which appears in living water states such as rain, natural springs, and within our own bodies. It can be measured, and the structure witnessed, as water freezes and unfreezes. Light appears to be the key to building this structured water. Dr Pollack's belief is that we function better with a negative charge in the body and environment, and that people should get more light in their lives to build more EZ cellular water, which will benefit health functioning.

EYE MOVEMENT DESENSITISATION AND REPROCESSING - EMDR

Eye Movement Desensitisation and Reprocessing is a technique used by therapists to treat distressing memories and associations linked to trauma and adverse life events. It is a form of psychotherapy developed in the 1980s by American psychologist Francine Shapiro.

When a person experiences something upsetting or traumatic, the brain may not process the memory as normal. In future, trauma can be triggered by smells or sounds for example, and people feel intense emotion linked to that hidden memory. An EMDR therapist guides the person through a systematic approach, often using left-right stimulation of the brain with eye movements, sounds or taps. The effect is thought to be similar to what occurs in the brain during REM sleep where our eyes move naturally from side to side. The premise is that making these rapid eye movements whilst recalling an adverse event or feeling is thought to activate the parasympathetic nervous system and trigger a calming feeling which then gets linked to the memory in the brain. The aim is not to get rid of the memory, but to make you care less about it; to feel it less. It is used especially when recalling events in detail would be too harrowing for a person, and can negate the need for many sessions of the talking therapies such as CBT. http://emdrassociation.org.uk/

FERMENTABLE OLIGOSACCHARIDES, DISACCHARIES, MONOSACCHARIES AND POLYOLS - FODMAPs

FODMAPs is an acronym that stands from Fermentable Oligosaccharides, Disaccharides, Monosaccharides and Polyols. They are all sugars and carbohydrate types found in many foods that we ferment in the gut. Some people have problems breaking them down, causing irritable bowel syndrome (IBS) type symptoms such as bloating, wind and upset bowel movements.

GUPTA PROGRAMME

A brain retraining programme developed by UK-based Ashok Gupta, who suffered from Chronic Fatigue Syndrome for three years and has been well for 15 years (2018). His research into the illness led him to conclude that these conditions involve the amygdala and insula in the brain and that they could be helped with amygdala-calming and neuroplasticity techniques. He runs a clinic and DVD/group programme teaching his techniques. https://www.guptaprogramme.com/

HYPERSENSITIVITY DISORDERS

This is a term I use to group together all types of chronic illness where people are over-sensitive in some way to triggers; where the brain, amygdala and central nervous system is somehow too turned up. The belief is that adverse childhood and later-life events affect the hippocampus, amygdala and other structures in the brain and nervous system that determine threats and safety; we become sensitised to stressors and can physically, mentally and emotionally over-react to what should be deemed safe. The aim in treatment is to re-set or lower the central nervous response. Central sensitivity syndrome also comes within this group and therefore conditions such as fibromyalgia, chronic pain and chronic fatigue syndrome.

MULTIPLE CHEMICAL SENSITIVITY - MCS

Multiple Chemical Sensitivity (MCS) is a condition whereby people become sensitised to chemicals in the environment, such as pesticides, perfumes or petrol fumes, or chemicals in toiletries, for example. It is distinct from multiple food sensitivity (MFS), where people are sensitive to several or many foods. Other people can be sensitive to electromagnetic fields (EMF) emitted by WiFi, mobile phone masts and mobile phones, for example. It is quite common for a hypersensitive person to be sensitive to one, two or all three. I then term this a hypersensitivity disorder.

NEUROPLASTICITY

In simple terms, this is the 'new' acceptance that our brains are not set in stone, as was previously thought, but can be changed. With every repetition of a thought or emotion, we build and reinforce neural pathways. Thinking the same things will make those neural pathways stronger over time and eventually they can become automatic. Our experience in life is directly shaped by our thoughts and our experience will shift and change as our thoughts do. Connections and synapses in the brain are constantly becoming stronger or weaker depending on what we do and think. Therefore, to change a habituated or chronic experience, we need to change the way we think about it. The plasticity – the ability of the brain to change – allows us to alter our experience by strengthening beneficial thoughts and weakening unhelpful ones. Check this video out for more on this: The Brain that changes itself.

NON-COELIAC GLUTEN SENSITIVITY - NCGS

Non-coeliac gluten sensitivity (NCGS) is a newly-recognised gluten disorder which is distinct from coeliac disease. There is much debate about it and new research is being conducted by many countries to understand it more fully. Our knowledge of it will evolve over time.

My clinical and personal experience so far is that it is the NCGS sufferers who tend to need the TrulyGlutenFree (TGF) approach and that they can be more sensitive to gluten and cross-contamination than coeliacs. NCGS sufferers have a different gene pattern and antibody markers, hence they are often missed by mainstream gluten illness tests, which look only for the most well-known coeliac markers.

Both coeliacs and NCGS can result in malabsorption syndromes, inflammatory and autoimmune diseases. You can find out more on NCGS here in my specialist section:
https://purehealthclinic.co.uk/trulyglutenfree/

PEAR ENLIGHTENMENT AND RELEASE - PEAR PROCESS

Personal Enlightenment and Release, was developed by hypnotherapist Olivia Stefanino. It is an audio programme that guides you through five steps to emotional wellness. These include the expression of emotion, forgiveness, acceptance, unconditional love and letting go. It is used most often as a way of finding repressed emotions that you may need to let go of to heal. http://www.pearprocess.com/.

PENNEBAKER'S METHOD

INVENTED BY DR JAMES PENNEBAKER, Chair of Psychology at Texas University, this is a method of expressive, therapeutic writing or journaling that Pennebaker's research in the 1970s found helped improve the health of the study participants. Many researchers have since corroborated this and there have been many clinical trials which show writing unconsciously and freely about how you feel somehow helps to stop people ruminating on the issues and to process them better, hence lowering stress and benefiting health.

QI GONG

ALSO KNOWN AS CHI KUNG, Chi Gung or QiGong, the literal translation is 'life energy cultivation.' It is practiced mainly in China, but throughout the world as a kind of movement meditation. The practice involves performing a set of slow, controlled, flowing movements with rhythmic breathing and a meditative state of mind.

REIKI MASSAGE

REIKI (RAY-KEY) MEANS 'UNIVERSAL LIFE ENERGY' in Japanese, and is a system of energy healing founded in 1922 by a Tendai Buddhist Monk and healer called Mikao Usui. It is now practiced in various adaptations throughout the world. A therapist is said to channel universal energy from a higher source into the person, although the system is not linked to any religious beliefs. Practically, the therapist can either touch or hover their hands over the patient's fully-clothed body. I think of it as massage for the aura, if you like. People either feel nothing, or distinct sensations, sometimes tingling, or see colours. It is very calming in most cases. The aim is to restore energy flow to encourage emotional and physical healing.

SILVA METHOD

Developed in the 1960s by US parapsychologist Jose Silva. Parapsychologists study paranormal and psychic phenomena. The Silva Method is practiced in almost 130 countries. It is described as a dynamic meditation technique, taught in-class or online, where people learn how to use guided imagery to help rewire the subconscious and retrain the brain. https://www.silvamethod.com/

STOPS

This is a common technique which I first came across in Dr Ashok Gupta's amygdala retraining programme for chronic fatigue sufferers. STOPs simply describes noticing as many times as you can what your inner voice is saying that is not helping you, literally saying 'stop, stop, stop' or a similar phrase to counter the inner voice, replacing it with something positive. Some people find saying 'stop', too harsh; I used humour to say 'aha, I saw that, that is not true any more'. I would then tell myself the opposite, for example, thinking I might react to a food, I would stop that thought and say 'that's not true; I can eat this food safely now,' or something similar. The repetition helps with neuroplasticity, building new neural pathways and ways of thinking.

TENSION MYOSITIS SYNDROME - TMS and TMS WIKI

Dr John Sarno coined the term Tension Myositis Syndrome (TMS) to describe a condition where chronic illnesses such as pain and fatigue syndromes were not caused by structural or biochemical problems that would show up in tests, but were the result of a mild lack of oxygen via the nervous system triggered by repressed emotions and stress. In other words, the symptoms were a direct result of the body trying to express repressed emotions.

If we try to suppress an emotion or feeling, we create a huge amount of emotional tension within the physical body. The body can then create pain or other symptoms as a distraction to help you not to focus on the emotional hurt. It is thought we develop this kind of symptom because we are unable to accept or process an emotional trauma of some kind. Treatment is designed to identify any repressed emotions linked to a condition, accept and process them, thus relieving any need for distraction illness.

The TMS WIKI is a website developed and written by TMS professionals, researchers and sufferers to raise awareness of this cause of common conditions like backache, migraine and fatigue, and suggests treatment options. http://www.tmswiki.org/

TRANSFORMATIVE WHOLISTIC REINTEGRATION - TWR

Transformative Wholistic Reintegration, formerly called WHEE (Wholistic Hybrid of EMDR and EFT) was created by Dr Daniel Benor, an American psychiatrist and MD. It combines elements of EMDR (Eye Movement Desensitisation and Reprocessing), a technique used for releasing trauma, and EFT (Emotional Freedom Technique) as above, used for releasing emotional triggers of illness.

Practically, instead of tapping on meridian points, you tap alternately anywhere on the body, most often using the so-called 'self-hug' where you tap your hands on the opposite upper arms. You can use your tongue on the roof of your mouth or tap your toes in your shoes. It can be done anywhere and in any situation very discreetly.

Similar to EFT, although a much simpler technique, it helps people release painful emotions and memories that may trigger illness or prevent healing, as well as helping to reduce physical symptoms, especially pain. It again combines verbalising certain phrases and talking through the issue, but has more emphasis on implanting more beneficial ways of thinking whilst you alternately tap. https://danielbenor.com/twr-app-home/

TRULY GLUTEN FREE - TGF

TrulyGlutenFree (TGF) is the phrase I coined to make a distinction between a traditional gluten free approach, which means avoiding gliadin, a protein and component of gluten present in wheat, rye and barley, and the truly gluten free approach, where someone needs to avoid all types of gluten, not just gliadin, and the cross-reactive gluten foods.

THERE IS a type of gluten in all grains and the body also reacts to other cross-reactive foods, such as dairy, as if it is gluten. My research suggested that many coeliacs on a traditional gluten free diet were not healing and my premise is that, in some people at least, they may have problems with the other forms of gluten and the cross-reactive foods. See my specialist section and book on this subject here: https://purehealthclinic.co.uk/trulyglutenfree/.

18

Further Resources

There are already links to all the key resources in the relevant steps of this plan. However, I've also gathered links to some of the most vital CDs, DVDs and books in the Mind–Body Medicine plan support space on my website – https://purehealthclinic.co.uk

IF YOU'D LIKE to do even more knowledge therapy and exercises, I heartily recommend the following:

NEUROPLASTICITY and the Brain

In Step Four, I recommended Dr Norman Doidge's 'The Brain That Changes Itself' as a crucial book to read. His other book, 'The Brain's Way of Healing: Stories of Remarkable Recoveries and Discoveries', is also excellent.

For more about the neurotransmitters and pain pathways in the brain, I recommend this paper—'The Science of Fibromyalgia'—by Dr Daniel Clauw, Dr Lesley Arnold and Dr Bill McCarberg.

I FOUND THE FOLLOWING USEFUL:

'The Power of Habit: Why We Do What We Do, and How to Change' by Charles Duhigg

'E-Squared: Nine Do-It-Yourself Energy Experiments That Prove Your Thoughts Create Your Reality' by Pam Grout

'Brain Rules (Updated and Expanded): 12 Principles for Surviving and Thriving at Work, Home, and School' by John Medina

DR LORIMER MOSELEY's TED talk, 'Why Things Hurt', is a very funny and interesting 15 minutes explanation.

EPIGENETICS

'The Genie in Your Genes' by Dawson Church

UNDERSTANDING YOUR SUBCONSCIOUS

'The Saboteur Within: The Definitive Guide to Overcoming Self Sabotage' by Matt Hudson

'The Power of Your Subconscious Mind' by Dr Joseph Murphy

'The Emotion Code' by Dr Bradley Nelson

'THE OBSTACLE IS YOU: The Manual You Should Have Been Given When You Were Born (How to Love Yourself Book 2)' by Munmi Sarma

TECHNIQUES

'Seven Minutes to Natural Pain Release: Pain is a Choice and Suffering is Optional—WHEE for Tapping Your Pain Away' by Dr Daniel J. Benor

'Pear Process: Personal Enlightenment & Release' by Olivia Stefanino

'Mindfulness for Health: A practical guide to relieving pain, reducing stress and restoring wellbeing' by Vidyamala Burch and Dr Danny Penman

Deepak Chopra's 'Chakra Balancing: Mind, Body & Soul' meditations are available on iTunes and Spotify.

MIND–BODY Medicine

'The Journey: A Practical Guide to Healing Your life and Setting Yourself Free' by Brandon Bays

'Quantum Healing' by Deepak Chopra

'Body Talk: Why You Really Get Sick and Why It Need Never Happen Again' by Rochelle Gordon

'Chronic Pain: your key to recovery' by Georgie Oldfield MCSP

'Change Your Mind, Heal Your Body: When Modern Medicine Has No Cure, The Answer Lies Within' by Anna Parkinson

'Molecules of Emotion: Why You Feel the Way You Feel' by Candace Pert

'The Fear Cure: Cultivating Courage as Medicine for the Body, Mind, and Soul' by Dr Lissa Rankin

'Mind Over Medicine: Scientific Proof That You Can Heal Yourself' by Dr Lissa Rankin

'You the Healer: The World-Famous Silva Method on How to Heal Yourself and Others' by José Silva

'Free to Love, Free to Heal: Heal Your Body by Healing Your Emotions' by Dr David Simon

'Meta Messages from Your Body: Discover the Cause of Disease and Why Your Body Doesn't Make Mistakes' by Sam Thorpe

Psychiatry

'Man's Search for Meaning: The classic tribute to hope from the Holocaust' by Viktor E Frankl

Philosophy & Spirituality

'Letting Go: The Pathway of Surrender' by Dr David R. Hawkins

'Being Here: Modern Day Tales of Enlightenment' by Ariel and Shya Kane

'The Wise Heart: Buddhist Psychology for the West' by Jack Kornfield

'The Untethered Soul: The Journey Beyond Yourself' by Michael A. Singer

'The Power of Now: A Guide to Spiritual Enlightenment' by Eckhart Tolle

Inspirational Stories

'Living the Journey: Using the Journey Method to Heal Your Life and Set Yourself Free' by Brandon Bays

'Breaking Night' by Liz Murray

Light Theory

'Light: Medicine of the Future' by Dr Jacob Liberman

Finally, don't forget to follow my Blog (https://purehealthclinic.co.uk/blog/) where I write about new healing techniques and tips that I've discovered, and do join the 'Healing Planners' Facebook group for people working this plan!

19

REFERENCES AND LINKS

ADVERSE CHILDHOOD EXPERIENCE - ACE

https://www.huffingtonpost.com/donna-jackson-nakazawa/childhood-trauma-leads-to_b_11154082.html?guccounter=1

https://www.nikigratrix.com/acescore/

https://acestoohigh.com/aces-101/

https://www.youtube.com/watch?v=j3ik_mm5YzE - Create Energy by Healing Trauma by Niki Gratrix

https://www.nikigratrix.com/healing-emotional-trauma-part-1-how-does-our-biography-become-our-biology/

https://www.nikigratrix.com/silent-aces-epidemic-attachment-developmental-trauma/

AMAZON BOOKS

If you enter these titles in the Amazon search box you should get taken to the books.

Davidji - Guided Meditations

The Artist's Way Workbook by Julia Cameron

Michele Rosenthal

Ariel & Shya Kane

The Body Keeps The Score by Bessel van der Kolk

Body Talk by Rochelle Gordon

The Brain's Way of Healing by Norman Doidge

Brain Rules (Principles for Surviving and Thriving at Work, Home and School by John Medina

Breaking Night by Liz Murray

Change Your Mind Heal Your Body by Anna Parkinson

Patricia Fennell

Georgie Oldfield MCSP

Dr Bradley Nelson

E-Squared: Nine Do-It-Yourself Energy Experiments That Prove Your Thoughts Create Your Reality by Pam Grout

Expressive Writing, Words that Heal by James W Pennebaker, PhD and John F Evans, EdD

The Fear Cure by Lissa Rankin, MD

Free to Love Free to Heal by David Simon, MD

The Genie in your Genes by Daswon Church, PhD

Michele Rosenthal

The Journey by Brandon Bays

The Last Best Cure by Donna Jackson Nakazawa

Letting Go The Pathway of Surrender by David R Hawkins, MD, PhD

Light Medicine of the Future by Jacob Liberman

Living the Journey by Brandon Bays

Man's Search For Meaning by Viktor E Frankl

Mindfulness for Health A Practical Guide to Relieving Pain, Reducing Stress and Restoring Wellbeing by Vidyamala Burch and Danny Penman

Mind Over Medicine by Lissa Rankin, MD

Molecules of Emotion The Science Behind Mind-Body Medicine by Candace B Pert, PhD

The Obstacle is You, Vol 2 by Munmi Sarma

Pathways to Pain Relief by Frances Summer Anderson & Eric Sherman

The Power of Habit by Charles Duhigg

The Power of Now by Eckhart Tolle

The Power of Your Subconscious Mind by Dr Joseph Murphy

Quantum Healing by Deepak Chopra

The Saboteur Within by Matt Hudson

Seven Minutes to Natural pain Release by Daniel J Benor

They Can't Find Anything Wrong! by David D Clarke, MD

The Untethered Soul by Michael A Singer

The Wise Heart by Jack Kornfield

You Can Heal Your Life by Louise Hay

You The Healer by José Silva and Robert B Stone

ANNIE HOPPER

https://www.youtube.com/watch?v=0_-nM2dHXMk - Annie Hopper Presentation

BEA RESNICK

https://www.youtube.com/watch?v=61cD7SAbm6Y - Bea Resnick

BRAD YATES

https://www.tapwithbrad.com/ - Brad Yates

https://www.youtube.com/watch?v=teQCBDlWKcw - Brad Yates - Beating Yourself Up

https://www.youtube.com/channel/UCiHZMZejDS4RIxDdBwoie9A - Brad Yates - Feeling As Good As Possible

https://www.youtube.com/user/eftwizard/search?query=acceptance - Brad Yates Self-Acceptance

https://www.youtube.com/watch?v=KHydpkmWydI - Brad Yates Self-Compassion

DANIEL BENOR

https://danielbenor.com/twr-app-home/twr-method/

My Book - Seven Minutes to Natural pain Release by Daniel J Benor

DR DANIEL J CLAUW

https://www.youtube.com/watch?v=pgCfkA9RLrM - Daniel J Clauw - Chronic Pain All In The Head

https://www.ncbi.nlm.nih.gov/pmc/articles/PMC3258006/ - Science of Fibromyalgia by Dr Daniel Clauw

DAVID CHILDERLEY

https://www.davidchilderley.com/?affcode=49672_tropzugi

https://www.davidchilderley.com/p/7-days-to-freedom?affcode=49672_tropzugi/

https://www.youtube.com/user/davidchilderley - David Childerley

https://www.youtube.com/watch?v=eQ5k9F3pSdo - David Childerley 30 Day Challenge For Self Acceptance

DAVIDJI

Davidji - Guided Meditations

Davidji - Guided Meditations, Fill What Is Empty, Empty

DEEPAK CHOPRA

https://itunes.apple.com/gb/album/chakra-balancing-body-mind-soul/57761960

https://open.spotify.com/album/59JPOCg3EQylr7zBevTmSl?autoplay=true&v=L - Chakra Balancing Body, Mind and Soul

https://chopracentermeditation.com/about-us

https://chopracentermeditation.com/store/product/2/perfect_health_streaming

https://itunes.apple.com/gb/album/chakra-balancing-body-mind-soul/57761960

Quantum Healing by Deepak Chopra

https://shop.chopra.com/21-day-meditation-challenge-perfect-health.html

DR DISPENZA

https://www.hayhouseu.com/making-your-mind-matter-online-course-hhu - Dr Dispenza

https://emofree.com/

https://evernote.com/

FACEBOOK GROUPS

https://www.facebook.com/groups/396815440703270/ - Healing Planners, Mind Body Medicine for Chronic Illness

https://www.facebook.com/groups/Trulyglutenfree/

GERALD POLLACK

http://www.danielvitalis.com/rewild-yourself-podcast/dr-gerald-pollack-on-the-fourth-phase-of-water

https://www.youtube.com/watch?v=Y--L6BoH3Ug - The Fourth Phase of Water by Gerald Pollack https://www.youtube.com/watch?v=kgvjBK93Ryo - Water Inside Us by Gerald Pollack

https://www.youtube.com/watch?v=bvDoOlX9Fn0 - Dr Mercola Interviews Gerald Pollack

Various

https://getpocket.com/

https://www.hindawi.com/journals/jeph/2012/291541/ - Grounding Article

https://www.ncbi.nlm.nih.gov/pmc/articles/PMC3258006/ - Science of Fibromyalgia by Dr Daniel Clauw

THE GUPTA PROGRAMME

https://www.guptaprogramme.com/

https://www.youtube.com/watch?v=c9wCUYxoZls&t=20s

https://www.youtube.com/watch?v=sHhRGC3GNXA - Gupta Programme Short Introduction

HEALING HISTAMINE

https://healinghistamine.com/

https://healinghistamine.com/the-anti-cookbook/

KLINGHARDT INSTITUTE

https://klinghardtinstitute.com/

https://klinghardtinstitute.com/wp-content/uploads/2015/06/HOME-PAGE-The5LevelsofHealing2.png

https://klinghardtinstitute.com/wp-content/uploads/2015/06/HOME-PAGE-The5LevelsofHealing.png

LISSA RANKIN

The Fear Cure by Lissa Rankin, MD

Mind Over Medicine by Lissa Rankin, MD

LOUISE HAY

http://alchemyofhealing.com/causes-of-symptoms-according-to-louise-hay/

You Can Heal Your Life by Louise Hay

MEDITATION OASIS

https://www.meditationoasis.com/podcast/

META HEALTH ACADEMY

http://www.metahealthacademy.com/

http://www.metahealthacademy.com/articles/meta-health-uncovers-the-cause-of-eczema-preview/

MICHELE ROSENTHAL

Michele Rosenthal

NATURAL DISPENSARY

https://naturaldispensary.co.uk/products/EFA_Sirt_Supreme_180_s-7455-0.html

https://naturaldispensary.co.uk/products/Multi_Vi_Min_150_s-4455-0.html

http://www.tmswiki.org/ppd/The_PEAR_Process

NORMAN DOIDGE

The Brain's Way of Healing by Norman Doidge

OPTIMUM HEALTH CLINIC

http://www.secretstorecovery.com

PATRICIA FENNELL

The Chronic Illness Workbook

THE PEAR PROCESS

CD, The Pear Process, Heal Your Past in Less than 1 Hour, with Olivia Stefanino

PENNY PRICE

https://penny-price.com/therapist-directory/

PSOAS RELEASE

https://www.youtube.com/watch?v=27cJTflmkMQ - Psoas Release for Stress and Backpain

PURE HEALTH CLINIC AND TRULY GLUTEN FREE

https://purehealthclinic.co.uk/category/mind-body-medicine/

https://purehealthshop.ecwid.com/Gluten-Autoimmune-and-Cyrex-Tests-p48202816

https://purehealthshop.ecwid.com/Gluten-Plan-p49344095?forcescroll=true

https://purehealthclinic.co.uk/the-gluten-healing-process/

https://purehealthclinic.co.uk/health-a-z/central-sensitivity-syndrome/

https://www.ecwid.com/store/purehealthshop/Mind-Body-Medicine-c20146257

https://purehealthshop.ecwid.com/Symptom-Checklist-p49365793

https://purehealthshop.ecwid.com/TGF-Supplements-Master-List-p49365828

https://purehealthclinic.co.uk/trulyglutenfree/

https://www.facebook.com/groups/Trulyglutenfree/

QI GONG

http://www.modernqigong.com/lp

DR SARNO

The Mind/Body Prescription

The Divided Mind: The Epidemic of Mindbody Disorders

SHEFFIELD YOGA

http://www.sheffieldyogaforme.org.uk/yogaNidraCD.php - Yoga Nidra

THE SILVA SYSTEM

http://www.silvamethod.uk.com/ - UK Site

http://www.silvalifesystem.com/ - US Site

http://www.silvalifesystem.com/free-lessons

VITAL AFFIRMATIONS

http://www.vitalaffirmations.com/health/health_af.htm#.WxqtzzNKib8

TOTAL RELEASE EXPERIENCE

https://treuk.com/who-is-tre-for/

https://www.youtube.com/watch?v=hTPFbd-5xmE&t=2118s - Introduction to TRE

https://www.youtube.com/watch?v=nmJDkzDMllc - Nature's Lessons in Healing Trauma

WIKI

http://www.tmswiki.org/w/index.php?page=The_Tension_Myositis_Syndrome_Wiki

http://www.tmswiki.org/ppd/An_Introduction_to_Tension_Myositis_Syndrome_(TMS)

http://www.tmswiki.org/ppd/TMS_Recovery_Program

YOUR HEALTH BASKET

https://www.yourhealthbasket.co.uk/index.php?l=product_detail&p=716

YOUTUBE

https://www.youtube.com/playlist?list=PLQATn4dKAnMRS4HKWhE9TZ6G2xZPqXZrj - 30 Day Challenges

https://www.youtube.com/watch?v=61cD7SAbm6Y - Bea Resnick

https://www.youtube.com/channel/UCiHZMZejDS4RIxDdBwoie9A - Brad Yates

https://www.youtube.com/channel/UCiHZMZejDS4RIxDdBwoie9A - Brad Yates - Feeling As Good As Possible

https://www.youtube.com/user/eftwizard/search?query=acceptance - Brad Yates Self-Acceptance

https://www.youtube.com/watch?v=KHydpkmWydI - Brad Yates Self-Compassion

https://www.youtube.com/watch?v=j3ik_mm5YzE - Create Energy by Healing Trauma by Niki Gratrix

https://www.youtube.com/watch?v=pgCfkA9RLrM - Daniel J Clauw - Chronic Pain All In The Head

https://www.youtube.com/user/davidchilderley - David Childerley https://www.youtube.com/watch?v=eQ5k9F3pSdo - David Childerley 30 Day Challenge For Self Acceptance

https://www.youtube.com/channel/UCj0VOmiaQPmnL1I2TauZ3ow - Dynamic Neural Retraining System

https://www.youtube.com/watch?v=sHhRGC3GNXA - Gupta Programme Short Introduction

https://www.youtube.com/watch?v=hTPFbd-5xmE&t=2118s - Introduction to TRE

https://www.youtube.com/watch?v=nmJDkzDMllc - Nature's Lessons in Healing Trauma

https://www.youtube.com/watch?v=27cJTflmkMQ - Psoas Release for Stress and Back pain

https://www.youtube.com/watch?v=Y--L6BoH3Ug - The Fourth Phase of Water by Gerald Pollack

https://www.youtube.com/watch?v=bvDoOlX9Fn0 - Dr Mercola Interviews Gerald Pollack

https://www.youtube.com/watch?v=kgvjBK93Ryo - Water Inside Us by Gerald Pollack

https://www.youtube.com/watch?v=gwd-wLdIHjs - Why Things Hurt by Lorimer Moseley

The Eight-Step Healing Path: Using Mind–Body Medicine to Recover from Chronic Illness

Edited by Hannah Lawrence

Designed & Published in 2018 by Berrydales Books